# MEETING OF MINDS

*A Way to Peace through Mediation*

'All Members shall settle their international disputes by peaceful means in such a manner that international peace and security, and justice, are not endangered."

*Chapter I, Article 2, paragraph 3*
*of the Charter of the United Nations*

# MEETING OF MINDS

*A Way to Peace through Mediation*

---

### BY ELMORE JACKSON

*Representative at the United Nations
of the American Friends Service Committee and
of the Friends World Committee for Consultation,
Lecturer in International Relations at Haverford College.*

---

With special contributions by:

CARL CHRISTIAN SCHMIDT
SIR FREDERICK W. LEGGETT

McGRAW-HILL BOOK COMPANY, INC.
New York    Toronto    London

1952

# MEETING OF MINDS
### *A Way to Peace through Mediation*

# *Foreword*

The book which Mr. Elmore Jackson offers us today has no need of a foreword. The author, knowing that one is never served better than by oneself, in an excellent introduction has taken care to explain to us the origin of his work, his aim, and even the method which he has followed in editing it. He has done this so simply and so clearly that we are fully informed of his intentions. Thus, it only remains for me to underline briefly the importance, the interest, and the usefulness of his effort. Mediation and conciliation are playing a greater and greater role in relations between classes and nations. This is fortunate. It is a manifestation of a tendency in which one can fully rejoice. It is an expression of one of the highest virtues which can be practiced: the desire to understand and be just toward one another.

Each time that one attempts to resolve a conflict without force one renders to men an enormous service in leading them in the path of wisdom and of respect for themselves and for each other.

All those who devote themselves to this task or who prepare themselves for it have a right to our esteem and our gratitude. It is logical that a mind interested in these problems of concilia-

v

tion will search to determine what there may be in common, as well as what differences exist, between social and international conciliation.

Mr. Jackson has treated his subject fully. It seems to me that he has left no aspect of it in the shadow, and he had the excellent idea of calling into collaboration men whose practical experience is considerable. This has given to the whole work an indisputable value and a very great interest.

What pleases me in this work is that the author, learned as he is, and knowing his subject so thoroughly, affirms, however, that mediation will never be a science but will always remain an art. In this I am fully in accord with him. If a man charged with re-solving a conflict, whatever it may be, does not possess certain almost indefinable qualities and a personality which inspires con-fidence, it is very probable that, whatever his good will, he will not succeed in his task.

In such a field, nothing can replace the human touch, so rare and so precious. But it is evident also that the man who is gifted and naturally apt in fulfilling this work of conciliation will find in the experience of others, and in the examination of cases and precedents, material upon which he can reflect at length and the study of which will eertainly enrich him.

In this field of conciliation, which is developing so rapidly in these days, Mr. Jackson has been able to bring to us a scholarly work which, however, avoids the exaggerations of the specialist. It is the work of an expert who remains a human being—a human type which is rather rare and very precious. This is an additional reason for me to wish the greatest success to this book.

*Paul-Henri Spaak*

# Acknowledgments

This book is, in itself, an experiment in the meeting of minds. To all of those who have joined in this inquiry the American Friends Service Committee and the editor would like to express their appreciation.

The greatest debt is obviously to those persons with successful and, in some cases, extensive experience in labor and international mediation who shared some of their insight and general experience in an initial meeting and then found the inquiry so stimulating that they participated in a series of subsequent group conferences.

Among those who joined in the initial meeting were Ralph J. Bunche, Director of the Division of Trusteeship of the United Nations and former Acting Mediator in Palestine; William H. Davis, former Chairman of the War Labor Board and presently Chairman of the Labor Relations Panel in Atomic Energy; Jesse Freidin, of Roosevelt, Freidin and Littauer; James N. Hyde, Special Assistant to the United States Representative to the United Nations; William M. Jordan, of the United Nations Secretariat; Arthur S. Meyer, then Chairman of the New York State Mediation Board; Clarence E. Pickett, Honorary Secretary of the American

Friends Service Committee; James T. Shotwell, Acting President, Carnegie Endowment for International Peace; William Simkin, labor arbitrator; Claude C. Smith, Philadelphia attorney.

As the discussions proceeded, the group was joined by Andrew W. Cordier, Executive Assistant to the Secretary-General, United Nations; Otto Klineberg, Professor of Psychology, Columbia University; Leo Malania, of the United Nations Secretariat; Theodore Paullin, of Connecticut; Miss Anne Simons, of the United Nations Secretariat; Donald B. Straus, labor mediator; George W. Taylor, of the University of Pennsylvania.

Different members of the group contributed memoranda which formed the basis of the further considerations. The main line of approach in the chapter dealing with the handling of labor disputes in the United States came from Jesse Freidin, William Simkin, and Donald B. Straus. A similar contribution was made by William M. Jordan and James N. Hyde to the section which deals with the mediation of international disputes. The part dealing with techniques in labor mediation grew out of contributions made by all of those from the labor field but especially the contributions made by William H. Davis, George W. Taylor, and Arthur S. Meyer. A special debt of gratitude is due to Donald B. Straus for his assistance in the preparation of Chapter 1 and to Mr. Straus and Francis Bradshaw for several of the suggestions for social science research included in Appendix II.

The responsibility for integrating these contributions as well as the final responsibility for the study has been taken by the editor. While at every stage the study has benefited from the group discussions and from the advice of the several people who have participated, the responsibility for its precise formulation must rest with the editor.

While the section on tentative conclusions was considered by the larger group, who felt that it constituted a body of ideas worthy of consideration, the responsibility for its wording and formulation rests with the editor, who is also responsible for the questions raised at the end. These questions were not discussed in any of the group conferences.

It was obvious that any comparative study of mediation in the labor and international fields should, in its labor sections, draw on a wider experience than that in the United States alone. It was thus with real pleasure that the American Friends Service Committee and the editor learned that Carl Christian Schmidt, who is in charge of mediation for the Royal Social Board in Sweden, and Sir Frederick W. Leggett, Chief Industrial Commissioner in Great Britain during the Second World War and British government delegate to International Labor Conferences for 14 years, were prepared to contribute chapters dealing with labor mediation and conciliation experience in their respective countries; and that Lois Jane Stone, a graduate of Columbia University's Russian Institute, was prepared to contribute the paper, included in Appendix I, dealing with labor-dispute settlement in the U.S.S.R.

Those who have been responsible for the study wish to express their special appreciation to the New Hope Foundation for the grant which made the study possible; to the Carnegie Endowment for International Peace for assistance in the publication arrangements; to Howard Wriggins, Anne Simons, Homy Jhabvala, and Evelyn Robin Barr for their editorial and other assistance; to Harry Shulman, who joined in one of the group conferences; to Elisabeth Jackson, whose deep interest in this inquiry has had at times to be matched by faith and a sense of humor; and to Elise Meager, Rudi Walton, and Ruth Allanbrook, whose skill at the typewriter and whose patience in dealing with various drafts have contributed so importantly to this study in human relations.

*Elmore Jackson*

# Introduction

The United Nations has had a fair measure of success over the past four years in the peaceful settlement of international disputes. The work of Count Bernadotte and Ralph Bunche in Palestine and of a United Nations Commission in Indonesia has been of outstanding importance. Out of these mediation efforts, out of measures taken by the United Nations in other situations which have helped bring hostilities to a close, as well as from other useful but less conclusive measures adopted by the Security Council or the General Assembly, a great deal of experience has accumulated as to those approaches which appear to facilitate and those which appear to hinder agreement.

Thus far United Nations experience in mediation has developed without direct reference to mediation in other fields. A special study was prepared by the United Nations staff of the experience of the League of Nations, but to date the United Nations has not explored mediation methods developed in other areas of conflict to see whether they have something to contribute to the development of its own efforts at peaceful settlement.

The proposal for this present study grew out of attendance at

United Nations meetings by Quaker observers who had some knowledge of labor-dispute settlement in the United States. As one watched the debates in the Security Council, and in certain committees of the General Assembly, one could not escape the conclusion that the general problems of securing agreement were somewhat similar in the two fields.

There is, for instance, the question of extended public debate by the conflicting parties. Is such debate an aid or a liability to early agreement? What relationship do public statements, and occasional public recriminations, have on the agreement-making process? Is there anything to be learned from the mediation and settlement of disputes of a lesser magnitude which would be of use in the handling of international disputes?

In many international disputes, following the general debate, the United Nations establishes a special commission, or appoints a single mediator, to handle the more intimate and detailed negotiations. Some of those persons who have been most successful in their international mediation work have had prior experience in labor mediation. Does this indicate only that the personal qualities which make for a mediator's success in both fields are very much the same, or does it mean that firsthand experience in one field is an aid to success in the other? Are the techniques for getting agreement in the two fields possibly somewhat similar? It is apparent that Mark Etheridge and Dr. Frank Graham, both of whom have served the United Nations with distinction, have in their international mediation work drawn heavily on their labor mediation experience. Dr. Graham was active in the settlement of labor disputes in the United States during the Second World War, and Mr. Etheridge has for several years been a member of the Labor-Management Committee in Louisville.

In his recent book, *A Modern Law of Nations*,[1] Philip C. Jessup

[1] The Macmillan Company, New York, 1949, p. 7.

suggested that "the parallelisms between labor relations within states and international relations among states are striking." Dr. Jessup goes on to suggest that it was experience in labor problems that led William Jennings Bryan, as Secretary of State, to negotiate a series of treaties providing for "cooling-off periods" and "fact-finding commissions." Ernest Bevin, the late British Foreign Secretary, suggested that industrial relations had much in common with international relations and that experience in the former field was a good guide to procedure in regard to disputes in the latter.[2]

There is thus a further query. There may be some similarity in the personal qualifications of mediators in the two fields, and even in the techniques useful in facilitating an agreement, but are there any similarities in the general types of mediatory bodies which are used in the two areas of conflict? Under what circumstances does the United Nations, and do those governmental authorities responsible for the settlement of labor disputes, appoint single mediators or three-member mediating commissions? Under what circumstances do they send out fact-finding commissions under instructions to mediate but also with the power, if their mediation fails, to make recommendations for settlement? Are some of the background considerations leading to these decisions the same?

It was clear that it would be at least worth while to explore further the parallels in the two areas. With this in mind Clarence Pickett, then Executive Secretary of the American Friends Service Committee, and Dr. James Shotwell, Acting President of the Carnegie Endowment for International Peace, invited several leading persons with experience in the mediation of labor disputes and a somewhat similar group with experience in the mediation

[2]Letter of May 26, 1950, to William H. Davis from Sir Frederick W. Leggett, British Labor Mediator.

of international disputes to join them for an initial discussion. The general line of inquiry proved so stimulating that a series of subsequent meetings were held. Out of these meetings this study has gradually taken shape. The purpose is to see if the experience in the two fields is sufficiently similar for the United Nations to profit in some way from the more extensive labor mediation experience. If similarities are found, that in itself would not suggest any easy transferability of experience. Even in the same field, no two conflicts are ever exactly the same.

There are obvious and striking dissimilarities in the settings in which labor and international disputes arise. While we are living in a world in which the idea that nations can pursue their foreign policy without reference to the international community is firmly challenged, this larger community as yet clearly lacks the established political and legal institutions in any sense comparable to those which the national community can bring to bear to restrain parties in conflict and to influence them toward some form of peaceful settlement. The parties to an industrial conflict are usually general partners in a single enterprise whose orderly continuance is of long-run advantage to both. While it can be argued that disputing states should for their own welfare resolve their disputes and practice good neighborly relations, the immediate advantages of such a course are seldom so persuasively apparent.

There would nevertheless appear to be sufficient parallels to make this inquiry a useful one. Disputes in both areas arise out of conflicts between powerfully organized groups whose relationships are not fully settled by law or contract and who are unwilling to have their interests subjected to the final and authoritative rulings of a third party. While in both the labor and international fields purely mischievous elements frequently play an important role in the creation or prolongation of conflict, these factors usually operate against a background in which the disputing groups believe vital interests (or at times survival itself) to be involved in the terms of any settlement. It is this concern for vital interests which causes the parties so vigorously to protect their freedom of action—even though such action might at times be painful to another group or to the wider community. It is thus that disputes in the two fields are appropriate for the processes of mediation; for it is of the essence of a mediated settlement that the parties in conflict, after appraising the available and practicable alternatives, are brought eventually to voluntary agreement.

In both the labor and international fields conflicts often involve a balance of power between the disputing groups. The parties may be of nearly equal strength or, more frequently, one may be in the ascendancy and the other in a position of trying to hold on to its power. In these latter cases the governmental agency, whether national or international, which is charged with responsibility for protecting the public interest, is faced with the problem of obtaining a solution before the forces reach the explosive point because of the too great rigidity of the holder of power.

The parallel between the two fields is accented because of the relative independence and highly developed self-consciousness of labor and management organizations in the "free economies" of Western political and economic institutions. These institutions have assumed that management and labor for the most part are free agents. Management feels it has the right to run its business very much as it sees fit. Labor insists that in the extreme case it must be able to rely upon its own power, exercised through the strike, to bring about a meeting of minds or to enforce its demands. Management has equally insisted upon its right to use its own power to break a strike and (within legal limits) to break a union—using a lockout if necessary. Although at a much lower place on the conflict scale, the resulting circumstances have certain general psychological and institutional similarities to the setting in which international disputes arise. We will be exploring both the similarities and dissimilarities further in the course of this study.

It will obviously be necessary for us to give substantial attention to the relationship between mediation and the institutional and power setting in which it takes place. For this reason we will discuss labor mediation and international mediation initially in separate sections. The groundwork for any conclusions can only be laid by our having a general but fairly comprehensive picture of the manner in which mediation is carried out in the two fields.

We will turn first to a discussion of labor mediation experience in the United States. That part of the initial chapter which deals with mediation techniques has grown out of a series of group discussions in which several of the leading United States mediators participated. Carl Christian Schmidt, who is in charge of mediation for the Royal Social Board in Sweden, has contributed a chapter on mediation in Sweden. Sir Frederick W. Leggett, Chief Industrial Commissioner in Britain during the Second World War, has written a chapter on the settlement of labor disputes in Britain. The paper prepared by Lois Jane Stone, dealing with the provisions for the handling of industrial disputes in the U.S.S.R., has only a limited relationship to the main course of this inquiry, but it is of sufficient general interest to justify its being included as an appendix.

We will not attempt any general interpretation of the legal powers either of the United Nations Charter or of the various legislative acts establishing the framework for the settlement of labor disputes. Our effort will be the equally if not more difficult one of discovering how the respective arrangements for mediation have worked in practice and suggesting some of the methods and techniques which have emerged as useful aids in the resolution of conflict. In Chapter 5 we will discuss further the similarities and dissimilarities in the two settings and suggest several areas in which it would appear that each of the two fields of peaceful settlement could profit from the experience of the other. Chapter 6 raises two questions of special importance in the further development of international mediation facilities.

Over many years a great deal of attention has been given to the means through which different types of conflict are resolved within the national community. As yet very little systematic attention has been given to the techniques and procedures which have been used in attempts to get agreement in difficult and emotionally charged international disputes. The international community has followed with great interest the mediation efforts of the United Nations and the debates which have surrounded them. There are daily evidences that peaceful settlement requires great patience and prolonged negotiation. If more were known, however, as to the reasons for success and failure in these efforts it might not only aid the United Nations in the development of its all-important peacemaking functions but, in addition, it might help all of us to see that process against the background of certain common experiences in human relations.

There is a highly individual quality about the approach of any mediator in his handling of a complicated dispute. The large number of varying factors in each conflict situation make any systematic study a hazardous task. Because of the number of variables it has been the conviction of many that mediation is, and must remain, an art and not a science. The present study makes no effort to reduce mediation to a science nor to a set of procedures likely to prove effective in all circumstances. The fact, however, that this exploration has progressed to the point at which an attempt is being made to present the basic material and some tentative conclusions in systematic form is an indication that those who have participated in the study have found what they believe to be important areas of common ground. If this preliminary investigation yields a substantial number of tentative conclusions it may be worth while for the exploration to be carried further and an attempt made to achieve a more complete analysis. If in its present form this study serves only to help mediators in both the international and the labor fields to see that there is a general body of experience on which they can draw, and as William H. Davis said in one of the group discussions, "to feel less lonely in their extremely difficult assignments," it will have served one useful purpose.

We will be dealing in this study primarily with the mediation of disputes. Conciliation is usually a more informal process and is closely related to the extension of "good offices." In the international field the terms "mediation" and "conciliation" have at times been used interchangeably. In both labor and international disputes, however, mediation is coming to be understood as that somewhat more vigorous process in which a third party has the freedom to serve as more than a go-between or chairman of negotiations and undertakes, if necessary, to suggest measures for possible settlement.

The section of the study dealing with the handling of international disputes is confined in the main to those conflicts which the United Nations has succeeded in getting into mediation. In the international field, as in the national field, major conflicts usually arise out of, or are aggravated by, unattended or unsolved minor ones. It therefore seems likely that the prestige and experience which the United Nations gains in solving the lesser conflicts will aid it in engaging its skill against the larger ones.

It may be useful to emphasize that this study deals with only one of the many ways through which the world can move toward the more orderly community desired by all. Through the economic, social, and trusteeship activities of the United Nations, through the work of the specialized agencies, and through regional organizations, programs of common action are being developed; and the point worth noting as particularly relevant to a study on mediation is that, as part of the normal process of such common action, every "functional" arrangement provides also for the mutual adjustment of claims and interests within the limits of that particular activity. In the more effective ordering of these economic, social, and political factors which so often combine in forming the basis of conflict, a setting is being created out of which more appropriate political institutions can grow. In a world, however, in which many areas are only now awakening to the possibility of economic and social development, the speed with which change is taking place is likely, if anything, to accelerate; and the clash of interests is likely to continue to outrun the political and economic institutions established as a means of dealing with it.

A great deal of attention is now being given to the ways in which the legal and political powers of the United Nations can be strengthened. It may be timely, therefore, to give serious consideration to this equally important and not unrelated activity of the United Nations—the peaceful settlement of disputes. The incalculable destruction of modern war bears testimony to the urgency of developing this side of the work of the United Nations.

# Contents

# MEETING OF MINDS
*A Way to Peace through Mediation*

# 1

## *The Nature and Handling of Labor Disputes in the United States**

In all the turbulent history of labor-management relations in American industry there has never been any nationally imposed compulsory arbitration of labor conflicts. Several states have passed laws providing for the compulsory settlement of disputes in public utilities, but both management and labor, even in periods of national emergency, have strongly and successfully opposed any such general legislative restriction on their freedom to take action which they might consider essential to the maintenance of their vital interests. Both groups have considered the risks to be too great in any such plan.

While the Federal government, in times of crisis, may have had

*This chapter was prepared with the special assistance of Donald B. Straus.

1

the ultimate authority to force some pattern of compulsory settlement of labor disputes, first management's, and then management's and labor's, power and independence have been such that
prudence and political considerations have dictated the development of other means of handling these conflicts.

An unusually varied and important body of experience has thus
been accumulated in the settlement of these disputes by methods
which do not remove from the parties the responsibility of voluntary agreement. In this section we will be examining these
methods.

### The Nature of Labor Disputes

We have suggested that present-day labor disputes arise between well-organized groups in the national community who
have been able to preserve for themselves considerable freedom
of action. Employees in the United States now have a legal right
to organize themselves into unions for the purpose of improving
wages, hours, and working conditions. If and when an agreement
is reached in such bargaining, it is put into a written contract.
These contracts between management and labor customarily extend for one year. Before the contract expires, negotiations are
usually undertaken for its extension on similar or modified terms.
The vast majority of such contracts are bargained out directly by
representatives of management and the union without assistance
from an outside "third party" or the coercive action of a strike.

If no agreement can be reached at the bargaining table, a deadlock in negotiations results and the normal sequence of events
leads either to a strike by the workers or, far more rarely, a lockout by management. These are the economic weapons of labor-
management conflict, and, as is frequently the case in other forms
of conflict, peace is usually restored only after both sides have
suffered economic losses. Fortunately, there have been developed

alternative procedures to the strike or lockout which often resolve apparently deadlocked negotiations without requiring the
dispute to pass through the open conflict stage.

In the negotiations around the bargaining table, and in any subsequent negotiations supervised by a mediator, those who represent labor and management must be careful to carry their constituencies with them. The union negotiator must think of his
standing in the next union election. He may need to keep in mind
the relationship of any proposed terms of settlement to those
achieved by a rival union. He will likely have to keep an eye on
the industry-wide interests of his union. The management representative is similarly far from being a free agent. He must take
into consideration not only the economic situation of the company, but also its industrial relations policies, and the industry-
wide implications of any terms agreed upon.

Because such negotiations are conducted on behalf of organized groups and yet are concerned with matters which involve for
both parties very personal questions of men's relationships to their
jobs and to their immediate livelihoods, they often take on a degree of intensity and emotional concern not present in other types
of conflicts within the national community. The average worker
gains a certain stake in his job. In Western democratic states employees have come to look upon their freedom to quit work as
one of their fundamental freedoms. As with other rights or freedoms believed to be fundamental, negotiations concerning them
often erupt into conflicts most difficult to solve.

**Two types of labor disputes.** Within the framework of man-
agement-labor negotiations, two very different types of labor disputes can arise.[1] One type is over the interpretation or applica-

[1]Disputes can arise over the initial recognition of the union by management and over the types of workers which the union may represent. The
National Labor Relations Board has jurisdiction over such disputes and

tion of an already signed agreement between the parties. This kind is the more numerous, but procedures for settling it have become widely accepted and successful. A large majority of labor contracts (approximately 90 per cent)[2] specify that any dispute over the interpretation or application of an agreement shall be submitted to arbitrators for final and binding decision. The arbitrator, in this instance, acts in the familiar role of a judge interpreting a particular law—the contract written by the parties through industry's legislative process of collective bargaining. In essence, the parties agree to lay aside the weapons of economic warfare for the duration of the contract and to replace them with a system of arbitration for settling all disputes which may occur under the terms of their basic agreement. Such arbitration arrangements may be provided for in the contract, may be established by the parties under a separate agreement, or may be created as an alternative to a strike at the time a deadlock occurs. A common denominator of all such arbitration arrangements is that the procedure is voluntarily accepted.

The other type of labor dispute, and the one which most frequently comes to the attention of the public, arises over the failure of labor and management to reach agreement on the terms of a contract or the extension of an existing contract. In only a few industries has arbitration machinery been established to cover such cases. In most of these disputes one or both parties, because of what they believe to be their vital interest, have been unwilling to commit themselves in advance to binding third-party settlement and have thus reserved their freedom of action.

---

must resolve them according to its interpretation of the Taft-Hartley Act. The handling of such disputes, which is a quasi-judicial procedure, is not described further in this discussion.

[2]*Monthly Labor Review*, U.S. Bureau of Labor Statistics, vol. 73, p. 39, July, 1951.

Since it is believed to be not only in the ultimate interest of the parties but also in the public interest that these more difficult disputes be settled without a strike or a lockout, and the incident interruption of commerce, the Federal government, some state governments, and occasionally city governments have provided mediation facilities to assist in their settlement. Our concern for the balance of this section will be with these disputes, usually difficult, that arise over a failure to agree on contract provisions.

**Labor conflicts in a free economy.** In the background of disputes between labor and management is the duty of government to maintain law and order. Riots and fist fights, or other violence which is likely to endanger the safety of the citizens, must be restrained or deterred by the use of the police.

A distinction can be drawn, however, between law and order in the physical and in the economic sense. In the United States, the use of the courts or of an injunction to restrict the right of the American worker to quit work has long been fought by labor and has, since 1932, been restricted by legislation. Any direct use of the police, beyond the maintenance of law and order, has been most vigorously opposed.

Before organized labor attained its present influence, direct governmental restraints were often employed to curtail union activity of any kind. Many unions enjoying collective bargaining rights today can recall that their organizing took place in spite of, and sometimes in the face of, governmental threats to use (or the actual use of) injunctions backed up by police power. Under these circumstances some unions have fought for their survival and lost; but many fought for survival and won.

After the First World War, a change took place in the climate of public opinion and the public gradually began to reject the idea of armed strikebreaking on the part of the government. Since the Norris-La Guardia Act of 1932, and especially since the passage of the Wagner Act in 1935, unionization in the United States has been protected by law, and the right to strike has been sanctioned at the same time that efforts have been made to bring strikes under approved rules of conduct. In the past, governmental efforts to suppress strikes by force had failed to produce industrial peace. If a new approach carried the risk of occasional economic disruption, the risk was thought not to be substantially greater (and possibly much less) than was involved in the use of the more forceful governmental measures previously employed. For the government to have persisted, in the face of growing union activity, in an effort to suppress strikes might well have led to further disruption of national life and the abandonment of the freedom for individual and group action which was believed essential in a free economy.

Out of painful experience governmental agencies and the general public have slowly learned that in circumstances in which men feel that their fundamental freedoms are violated, the threat of armed governmental intervention rarely if ever creates the conditions essential to the settlement of industrial conflicts. The more serious labor disputes are so highly charged emotionally that the threat to invoke some type of court or police action usually serves to aggravate the conflict and to lessen the possibility of the government facilitating an early settlement by other and more effective means. Bitter experience has shown that this is just not the way in which industrial conflicts are settled.

To say this, however, is not to lessen the importance of these same instruments of government in helping to establish community respect for law and in underwriting an orderly framework of national life within which other modes of industrial settlement can be developed. Nor is it to suggest that national governments do not have the ultimate power and, in fact, the responsibility to attempt to maintain the continuation of production and of public facilities in times of national emergency or in periods in which the national safety appears to be threatened. If police action is too blunt an instrument for dealing effectively with industrial conflict situations in which workers' and management's fundamental freedoms seem to them to be at stake, it exists as one of the stabilizing elements in the political setting in which the conflict takes place. As a symbol of the general power of the organized community, it is one of the factors to be reckoned with in the adoption of any course of action likely to lead to the disruption of public order.

**The concept of public interest.** Supplemental to the power of the national community to maintain law and order, and indeed undergirding it at many points, is the gradual recognition in national life of the supremacy of the "public interest." The paramount nature of this public interest is more obvious in time of national emergency. However, rapid technological progress and the resultant interdependence within the national economy have made many types of industrial disputes, which formerly concerned only a small segment of the community, now a matter of general public concern. In this connection one has only to mention the wide repercussions of major strikes in the coal or steel industries. The growth of the concept of public interest has been slow, but the recognition of it has now reached the point where it is one of the factors which must usually be weighed by a union before calling a strike, or by management when adhering to a position that will precipitate a strike.

The public is chiefly concerned with the maintenance of production or public services. If the dispute is in the coal industry, the public wants to be assured that its homes will be kept supplied with heating fuel, and that the wheels of industry will not be halted by a lack of coal. If the dispute is in a transit company, the public is concerned with the inconvenience of travel to stores and to work. Of special concern to the government are disputes which interfere with defense production.

The public interest may also be concerned with the nature of the settlement which ends a strike. Recent wage-stabilization policy recognizes that a pay increase which threatens to increase inflation is contrary to the national welfare, even if it appears to be the only way to keep the men at work. Even in relatively "normal" economic periods, the public will display concern over agreements which hint at collusion between management and the union at the expense of the consumer or which otherwise appear harmful to the economy.

Many of the more serious labor disputes occur in times of major economic readjustment. These major economic changes are usually related to fluctuating tides of economic and organizational power. Industrial history offers many examples of rigid arrangements for settlement which fail to survive these economic upsets. The mediation process has the advantage of providing a flexible but orderly framework within which the changed circumstances of the parties can be adjusted under the general supervision of the public interest.

Whether or not the parties in particular disputes recognize the existence of the public interest, the probability that the government will intervene in its behalf if a strike creates a national emergency is undoubtedly a factor which influences the participants in industrial disputes to seek a settlement by mediation. As the national economy operates through larger and more interdependent units, critical situations appearing to justify governmental intervention become continually more numerous.

### Types of Machinery through which Settlement Is Attempted

**Mediation and arbitration.**  There is a spectrum of action which can be taken by an impartial person or group in attempting the settlement of a labor dispute. This ranges all the way from carrying messages back and forth between the parties in conflict to the issuance of an award which they must accept. There are many terms used to define the various gradations of this spectrum[3] but two major divisions are in common use: mediation and arbitration.

A single mediator's role usually extends up to, but does not include, the issuance of recommendations or awards. He may exert his efforts to bring the parties together in conference, he may seek clarification of the issues and aid in their interpretation, he may even suggest possible solutions. But in a labor dispute a mediator usually exceeds his authority if he makes public his suggestions or otherwise attempts to bring public pressure to bear upon the parties. This limitation upon the activities of a mediator minimizes the risk to either party of being forced into a settlement which it would not voluntarily accept.

Occasionally a mediator is given the power to make public his findings or even to announce his recommendations for a settlement if his mediation efforts fail to produce agreement. While either party may refuse to accept the suggestions, the mere fact of their publication may result in public pressure for their acceptance.

An arbitrator's function is to hear the facts and arguments of a case and to issue an award which is binding upon the parties. Voluntary arbitration occurs when the parties agree in advance to submit a particular dispute, or disputes of a certain category, to this method of resolution. If arbitration is accepted, the parties retain the freedom of choosing the arbitrator, and of stipulating

[3]The full spectrum runs: mediation without a public report, mediation with a public report, fact finding without a report, fact finding with a public report, fact finding with public recommendations, arbitration with an unenforceable award, arbitration with a binding award.

the issues he shall decide and the procedures he shall follow in making his decision. But once arbitration is entered into, both sides must accept its outcome, unless, as in an occasional case, the parties agree to have the arbitrator make a nonbinding award.

The term "compulsory arbitration" implies that when this method of settling disputes is used it is imposed from the outside. Under compulsory arbitration the parties must submit to the prescribed method of settlement, and they have very little discretion over the issues to be decided, who shall decide them, and the procedures which shall be followed. We have noted that a few states have passed compulsory arbitration laws concerning public utilities. Otherwise it is a form of arbitration not generally used in the United States.

Mediation has now achieved widespread acceptance in the United States as a proper method for attempting to settle labor disputes. Most labor disputes, no matter where they arise, or in what industry they are, will be subjected to mediation before they result in open conflict.

The type of initial mediation that any particular dispute will receive depends upon the industry in which it arises, whether or not it affects interstate commerce, and the probable effect of a strike upon the community. Most mediation is undertaken by agencies of the Federal government, or of state or local governments. Much of it is performed within the framework of specific legislation. Occasionally private mediation machinery is established by the parties.

The principal types of mediation machinery currently in use are described below.

**Voluntary arrangement of the parties.** Occasionally the participants in a labor dispute will prefer to select a particular individual to act as mediator, rather than to accept the services

of a government agency. The variety of circumstances out of
which such a decision may arise are infinite. In some cases the individual selected may be the one who serves as the permanent
arbitrator of the company or industry and who handles their
grievance disputes, or he may be a government official.

**Federal Mediation and Conciliation Service.** While the Federal government has maintained since 1914 an agency for the
mediation of industrial conflicts, the present Federal Mediation
and Conciliation Service was created under Title II of the Labor
Management Relations Act of 1947 (often referred to as the Taft-
Hartley Act). The jurisdiction of the Federal Mediation and
Conciliation Service is similar to that of the Act itself: it may
mediate any dispute between an employer and his employees
when the conflict affects interstate commerce, with the exception
of railroad and airplane transportation, which is covered by the
Railway Labor Act. The Service may enter a dispute upon its
own initiative or upon the request of either party, but it is
directed to avoid disputes which have only a minor effect on
interstate commerce. The law provides that the Service be informed of a labor dispute 30 days or more in advance of the date
on which an existing contract may be reopened. This provision
is designed to warn the Service of any potential dispute which
may eventuate in a strike, except, of course, for "wildcat" strikes
which do not have the sanction of the responsible union leadership. Managements and unions are obligated to participate in
any mediation sessions called by the Service.

The Service maintains a national office in Washington and 12
regional offices throughout the country. In 1951 there were a total
of approximately 200 Commissioners (mediators) attached to the
regional offices, each of whom was available for mediation work
on the assignment of his Regional Director. The Regional Directors keep in close touch with the industrial activity in their areas

and the initial efforts to settle a dispute are usually made from the regional office.

The Regional Director reviews notices of disputes and decides on the basis of the information available to him whether or not the Service should "enter the dispute." The decision will depend upon such factors as the effect of a strike on interstate commerce, and the size and importance of the company. Should the decision be made that the dispute does not come within the jurisdiction of the Service, the notice is filed without further action.

When the Service has accepted jurisdiction in a case, a Commissioner is assigned and is required to report to the Regional Director at regular intervals as to the progress that has been made and the manner in which he is participating or assisting in the negotiations.

If the parties are making satisfactory progress toward settlement, the Commissioner will refrain from active participation in the negotiations. In an active case the Commissioner takes the initiative, meeting with the parties jointly or separately as circumstances suggest. In some instances assignments are made to two or three Commissioners to sit as a mediation panel.

Should the dispute not be settled on the regional level it is referred to the national office. One or more Federal mediators are then assigned to the case, or, if the dispute is of sufficient importance, the Director of the Federal Service may enter the case.

The timing of intervention by the national office depends very much on the nature of the industry and the circumstances of the dispute. In some of the larger industries where a dispute may threaten to disrupt a substantial segment of the economy, the regional office of the Service makes little effort to settle the case but quickly refers it to the national office. In other cases a more prolonged effort is made on the regional level. In these cases, if the dispute is a particularly difficult one, the closest contact is maintained between the regional and national offices.

Should the national office fail to effect a settlement, and if the Director believes that a resulting strike may threaten the "national health and safety," he must notify the President who may then decide to attempt some form of emergency settlement.

**State mediation machinery.** Several states which have concentrations of industrial activity have established State Mediation Boards to aid in the voluntary settlement of disputes. Section 8 (d) (3) of the Federal law recognizes the state machinery by requiring employers and unions to notify existing state mediation agencies of an impending dispute, as well as to notify the Federal Mediation Service.

New York State is probably the most advanced in the development of this type of state mediation activity. The Board members are appointed by the Governor. The activities of the Board and the mediation procedures which it follows are in general similar to those of the Federal Mediation and Conciliation Service.

If mediation fails, New York law has provided a further step which can be taken. The State Industrial Commissioner may appoint a "Board of Inquiry" to handle a dispute which is a potential danger to the citizens of the state. Under the law the Board of Inquiry must make a final report to the State Industrial Commissioner. At the discretion of the Board of Inquiry the report may or may not contain a recommendation for the settlement of the dispute. Since the passage of this law in 1941, only one Board of Inquiry has ever heard a case. After a week of hearings, the Board of Inquiry was able to persuade both parties to submit all issues to arbitration before a panel consisting of the five members of the Board of Inquiry.

**City mediation machinery.** Several cities have established mediation services to handle disputes affecting the welfare of the community. In most instances a special office has been created by the Mayor for this purpose. Occasionally a group of prominent and public-spirited citizens, whose prestige can arouse the pressure of public opinion if necessary, have created an organization out of which mediators are provided when there is threat of a local labor crisis.

**Mediation plus the power to recommend.** In those types of machinery discussed thus far the mediators are usually confined, either by the law under which they operate or else by arrangement of the parties, to the role of getting agreement. If they fail in their mission, the usual result is a strike. In recent years the continuing production of an increasing number of industries has become so important to the national welfare that the weight assigned to the evil of governmental intervention has somewhat diminished in comparison to that of a strike. Accordingly, labor relations experts have sought strike-prevention methods that may be more effective than mediation alone, even at some sacrifice to the prerogatives of management and labor. One device that has been both popular and comparatively successful has been to give the mediator the power to issue recommendations for the settlement of a dispute should his mediation efforts fail.

The mediator's report is usually directed to a superior governmental authority or to the public. In such cases there are frequently three or more men on the mediation board. The reporting responsibility of these bodies often is emphasized to a greater extent than that of mediating.

The underlying purpose in giving such a board the power to issue a report is to bring to focus the full weight of public opinion upon the parties. It is the hope that, faced with this new power factor, the parties will decide to abandon the positions which have made agreement impossible.

The report can be limited to the presentation of facts, or its scope can be extended to embrace recommendations or the assessment of blame. A recommendation is, of course, a more powerful instrument to bring about an eventual settlement than a recital of facts. On the other hand, there are some experienced mediators who feel that an ultimate power to issue recommendations can seriously limit the effectiveness of a mediator in his primary role of obtaining agreement around the bargaining table.

Subscribing to this belief are those who feel that a mediator should not concern himself with his own judgment of the merits of a case. His job, according to this school of thought, is to preserve and advance the opportunities of the parties to settle the dispute on the basis of the merits and the practical necessities, as the parties can be brought to appraise them.

The Railway Labor Act machinery and the Atomic Energy Labor Relations Panel are two mediation bodies with report-issuing powers.

*Railway Labor Act machinery.* The Railway Labor Act is one of the oldest pieces of labor legislation in existence in the United States, and has been the product of joint discussions of management and labor representatives. The current Act was adopted in 1934. In 1940 the provisions of the Act were extended to cover the air-line industry.

The Act establishes elaborate mediation machinery for the settlement of disputes. It provides that an employer shall not, without the agreement of the union, "change the rates of pay, rules, or working conditions of its employees," and that employees shall await the exhaustion of the established mediation machinery before resorting to strike.

For the settlement of disputes over the interpretation of contracts the Act establishes four national Boards of Adjustment, composed of an equal number of employer and employee representatives. If agreement is not reached the Board selects a neutral person who hears the case and casts the deciding vote. If the parties themselves cannot agree upon the neutral person, then the National Mediation Board (whose activities are described below) makes the selection.

Unionization on the railroads has a long history, and the collective bargaining relationships have become complicated and sophisticated. The working rules embodied in the agreements are extremely detailed, and give rise to many disputes over their interpretation. As a result, the case loads of the various Boards of Adjustment have, in recent years, become excessively heavy. A case backlog of three years or more is commonplace.

As a consequence, the unions in recent years have, on several occasions, attempted to bypass the cumbersome machinery of the Adjustment Boards by turning disputes, which would normally be handled as grievances under a contract, into disputes over a change in the contract itself. This has put the Railway Labor Act in danger of a complete breakdown.

The Railway Labor Act established a National Mediation Board to mediate disputes not covered by contract. One or both parties may refer a dispute to the Mediation Board or the Board may proffer its services in case an emergency is found to exist. If mediation fails, no change in wages or working conditions may take place for 30 days. During this period the union may take a strike vote. If the result of the vote is in favor of a strike, and if, in the judgment of the Mediation Board, such a strike would "threaten substantially to interrupt interstate commerce to a degree such as to deprive any section of the country of essential transportation services," the Board must then notify the President who may, in his discretion, create an Emergency Board.

Railway Emergency Boards usually number three persons, all chosen by the President as impartial people representing the public. Such Boards are directed to investigate disputes and submit recommendations for their settlement.

Following the appointment of such a Board, and for a period

of 30 days thereafter, neither party may disturb the *status quo* or do anything which will interrupt transportation services. The recommendations of the Emergency Board are not binding on either party, and should either refuse to accept the recommendations, then the Railway Labor Act machinery has run its full course and a strike may legally take place.

For at least 20 years following the enactment of the Railway Labor Act, it was considered a model piece of legislation. It was originally written in full consultation with the railroad companies and the labor brotherhoods and as a result received their wholehearted acceptance. With a few noteworthy exceptions, the machinery embodied in the Act maintained peace on the railroads throughout this period.

Within the last few years, however, even the emergency machinery of the Act has been severely tested. Some strikes have occurred. In several instances the President has sought to invoke "extra emergency" methods. In one instance, he threatened to recommend to Congress that legislation be enacted permitting him to draft railway workers into the Army. This threat was never put to the test. The railway brotherhoods called off the strike almost before the words announcing the threat had left the President's lips. Public reaction to the threat of drafting striking railway workers into the Army was unfavorable, and this procedure has not again been seriously contemplated.

On a more recent occasion, the President has "seized" certain railroads and put them under the operation of the Army. In spite of this, some work interruptions have occurred, even though the strikes were now theoretically illegal because they were technically against the government as "employer."

These recent events have caused debate in Congress concerning possible revisions of the law. A bill was offered during the summer of 1950 by Senator Forrest Donnell, Republican of Missouri, which would make it mandatory for the parties to accept the recommendations of a Presidential Emergency Board. Considering the traditional position of management in respect to compulsory arbitration, it is interesting that the carriers favored this measure. The unions, however, opposed it and the bill was defeated.

*Labor Relations Panel in Atomic Energy.*  The atomic-energy plants are operated by private contractors, but with government funds and under over-all supervision and planning of the government. During the Second World War the Army was the government agency in charge of the program. Because of security considerations, collective bargaining was not allowed. After the war, the atomic-energy program was placed under a civilian agency and the ban against unionization was lifted.

Within a short time, unions had organized most of the plants. During the summer of 1948 a deadlocked negotiation at Oak Ridge threatened to interrupt activity in this important atomic-energy facility. A Taft-Hartley injunction was invoked but when the 80-day period had passed the dispute was still unsettled. The government resorted to extraordinary pressures to keep the men on the job. The Atomic Energy Commission told the workers that should they walk out, the government would replace them with a sufficient force to keep the laboratory going; in short, if necessary, the government would resort to the use of strikebreakers. At the same time, the AFL Council put pressure on the disgruntled workers to remain at work. This was a combination of antistrike measures which could work once under a crisis situation but which, over the long run, provided no basis for the orderly settlement of disputes.

The President therefore appointed a Commission to study the problem. The report of the Commission recommended the establishment of a Labor Relations Panel with the power to mediate disputes and to issue recommendations for their settlement. In

April, 1949, the Atomic Energy Labor Relations Panel was established. The final recommendatory powers of the Panel are similar to those of the Railway Mediation Board described above. There is, however, one interesting difference. The Panel has no statutory base. The Atomic Energy Commission and the unions were consulted fully about its establishment, and it relies wholly upon the voluntary acceptance of its mediation activities by the parties concerned. Public opinion, plus the realization by the parties that interruption of production in the atomic-energy program is not an available alternative, are the main forces which keep the Panel in business.

The absence of a law governing the activities of the Panel permits it to operate far more informally than does the Railway Mediation Board. When either a company or a union, or the Atomic Energy Commission itself, feels that a dispute may result in a strike, the Panel is notified. Usually the first action of the Panel is to have one of its staff investigate the background of the dispute, attempt to clarify the issues, and with this factual background make a report to the Panel members. If the report indicates that the parties have made a genuine attempt to reach accord through their own efforts, and, in addition, have fully utilized the Federal Mediation and Conciliation Service, then the Panel will assume jurisdiction of the case. If, on the other hand, the evidence shows that the parties have not fully exhausted their own resources to bargain, then the Panel may so inform them and request that they resume their negotiations before again applying for Panel assistance.

If the Panel takes a case, one or more Panel members are assigned to it. The first step is mediation. The Panel is bound by no rules and, as a matter of fact, in its brief history has followed no set pattern for attempting to obtain agreement. If the Panel's efforts fail to achieve agreement, it will then obtain whatever additional information it feels it needs, and proceed to issue recommendations. At no time during these procedures are strikes forbidden by law.

During its first year of activity, the Panel was able to settle most of its cases without issuing recommendations. More often, however, it has been necessary to issue recommendations in many of the cases in which its services have been invoked. Up to the present, all of these recommendations have been accepted by the parties.

**National emergency machinery.** Each year several industrial disputes defy settlement through the regularly established channels and, in one way or another, threaten to disrupt some important sector of the national economy. When this occurs, the President must exercise his power to prevent a disaster. Recently, Presidential emergency powers have been used either through an injunction, as provided for in the Taft-Hartley Act, through special Fact-finding Boards, or by government seizure.

*Taft-Hartley injunction.* The Taft-Hartley Act provides a set of "national-emergency procedures" which may be instituted if mediation fails to settle a dispute. These may be summarized as follows:[4]

1. "When 'in the opinion of the President,' a situation exists which threatens the 'national health and safety,' he may appoint a Board of Inquiry to make a written report to him within a specified time. The report, to be made public, is not to contain any recommendations.
2. "Following receipt of the report, the President 'may direct' the Attorney General to petition an appropriate District Court to enjoin the actual or threatened stoppage.
3. "The court has jurisdiction to enjoin such stoppage if 'the court

[4]*Federal Fact-finding Boards and Boards of Inquiry*, p. 2, U.S. Department of Labor, Bureau of Labor Statistics, Washington, D.C.

finds' that it affects an entire industry or substantial part and would imperil the national health or safety.

4. "The court injunction introduces an 80-day waiting period during which 'it shall be the duty of the parties to the labor dispute . . . to make every effort to adjust and settle their differences' with the assistance of the Federal Mediation and Conciliation Service established by the Act.

5. "In the case of unsettled disputes, the President reconvenes the Board of Inquiry which submits its final report by the sixtieth day describing the parties' current position, their efforts at settlement, and the employer's last offer. Again, no recommendations are to be made.

6. "The NLRB takes a secret ballot of the employees within the next 15 days to determine 'whether they wish to accept the final offer of settlement made by their employer.'

7. "Within the last five days, the NLRB certifies the results to the Attorney General, who then requests and obtains a discharge of the injunction from the court. The parties are then free to take any action they see fit.

8. "The President is required to submit a full report of the proceedings to Congress with any recommendations he may choose to make."

Although these provisions were intended to bring substantial reserve powers to bear in support of, or supplementary to, mediation efforts, in actual practice the emergency provisions of the Taft-Hartley Act have proved to be ineffective. Although the injunction itself has in several instances been successful in stopping a strike for the 80 days, there is no adequate provision for a stepping-up of the mediation process during the no-strike period. In many instances the dispute has gone through the period of injunction without solution and emerged on the other side with a renewal of strike activity.

*Fact-finding Boards.* We have noted that under the Taft-

Hartley Act the President is empowered to appoint a Board of Inquiry in connection with any strike or lockout in which mediation has been unsuccessful and which is likely to imperil the national safety or health. The report of the Board is made public but the Board itself may not make recommendations. Similarly the New York Mediation Board may certify to the Industrial Commissioner that a labor dispute vitally affects the public interest. Under these circumstances the Commissioner is empowered to approve a Board of Inquiry which may issue a factual report or may make recommendations.

Federal Boards of Inquiry were appointed in seven disputes during 1948 and one in 1950. In three cases all the steps provided for in the national-emergency provisions of the Taft-Hartley Act were used and in two cases strikes subsequently occurred. In one case all the provisions of the Act were used and the President finally recommended to Congress that a government seizure take place. This case was settled, however, before such action was authorized.[5]

More recently the President has seen fit in most instances to establish nonstatutory fact-finding and mediatory boards similar in nature to those employed with some success immediately after the Second World War. The boards are appointed under the President's general powers and are free to make recommendations.

Between 1945 and 1950 a total of 16 such Federal Fact-finding Boards were appointed. Six cases were resolved without work stoppages. In 11 cases board recommendations were accepted either fully or with minor modifications. In all 16 cases the recommendations had an important bearing on the terms of the settlement.[6]

Such boards represent the creation on an emergency basis of a

[5] *Ibid.*, p. 3.
[6] *Ibid.*

type of combined mediating-reporting to which we referred in connection with the work of the Labor Relations Panel in Atomic Energy and the Railway Labor Act. Boards of this kind are frequently employed in major conflicts in the coal and steel industry, in the communications industry, or in other industries in which the public interest is heavily involved. Fact finding has a tendency to narrow down and shape the area of negotiation. The general power which such boards possess has made their work at times a first cousin to compulsory arbitration.

The practice of having Federal mediatory and fact-finding boards empowered to issue recommendations for settlement is further extended in the President's executive order of April 2, 1951, establishing the Wage Stabilization Board. In cases which threaten an interruption of work affecting the national defense the Wage Stabilization Board is authorized to take jurisdiction (1) if the parties jointly agree to submit the case to the Board and be bound by its decisions and (2) if the President is of the opinion that the dispute substantially threatens the progress of national defense and certifies the dispute to the Board. In such cases the Board is empowered to report to the President on the issues in dispute with its recommendations to the parties for a fair and equitable settlement.

*Government seizures.* A frequently used restraint in the public interest has been the government seizure of plants or of facilities, or the threat of such governmental seizure, in order to keep production going, or facilities serving the public in operation, pending a settlement of the issues in dispute. This device was employed by President Wilson once during the First World War and was both threatened and undertaken several times during the Second World War. It has been used in one railway strike since and has been threatened in others and in one coal strike. The threat of government seizure has at times been sufficient in postwar public-emergency disputes to cause the parties to modify their claims and agree to proposals suggested by the mediator.

On the other hand, there have been occasions when government seizure, rather than being useful as a governmental threat, has actually been urged by one of the parties.

Once the government has seized a plant, there is a presumption based on past experience that the workers will return to work. At this point, there are two alternative ways toward an eventual settlement: (1) the government may negotiate a settlement directly with the union and then offer the plant back to the private owner for operation under new contract terms, or (2) the parties themselves may resume direct negotiations while the plant is in the hands of the government with the understanding that the plant will be returned to the owner once an agreement is reached. In one recent railroad dispute, the case remained unsettled and a work stoppage occurred as much as five months after government seizure. It would thus appear that even this method of governmental restraint does not in itself provide any final assurance against an interruption of production or of public services.

### General Practices and Techniques in Mediation

Mediation deals with human variables and therefore is not susceptible to any rigid set of rules. In the course of several conversations at Quaker House, a group of men with wide experience in the practice of labor mediation were able to distill from their experience some general guideposts in the approach to mediation and for a mediator's conduct. The following section describes these guideposts roughly in the order in which they would be used. Although no one case would fit into this pattern, the points made here should be suggestive of the present state of the "art and science" of labor mediation.

**Adapting the mediatory machinery to the particular dispute.** In the preceding sections we have outlined briefly the principal types of regular governmental facilities which have been established for dealing in the initial stages with labor disputes in the United States. Most industrial conflicts which become matters of general public concern do so only after they have defied early settlement through one or more of these agencies.

Although the statutory and institutional arrangements are generally fixed, the actual approach to mediation varies a great deal within the particular framework in which the dispute receives initial treatment. The mediatory personnel and specific procedures, especially in the more difficult cases, are selected with an eye to the peculiarities of the dispute. In handling difficult disputes at both the regional and national levels the selection of personnel and of procedure is usually made in close consultation with the parties to the dispute. There is usually a direct relationship between the outcome of the mediation effort and the degree to which the particular arrangement for mediation is developed in such a way as to gain for it the initial confidence of the parties.

**Selection of the mediator.** Confidence in the wisdom and impartiality of the proposed mediator, and in the arrangements for his selection, are important factors leading to the acceptance by the parties in dispute of any suggested form of mediation. This is presumably just as true with regard to any advance representatives of the mediatory agency as it is with regard to a fully empowered mediator who might eventually be appointed.

The principal attributes of a good mediator in the labor field would appear to be:[7]

1. A conviction that an agreement of the parties is better than an outsider's solution.

[7]From a memo prepared in connection with this study by William Simkin, wartime Chairman of the War Labor Board Shipbuilding Commission.

2. A personal knowledge of the industry, a knowledge of the history of its labor relations, and a sympathetic understanding of the issues in dispute.
3. Ability and experience in quickly analyzing both factual and human data.
4. Patience, tempered by a talent for sensing when one step should be terminated and the next step initiated.
5. A fertile and imaginative mind for devising alternative solutions.
6. The ability to "sell" alternative solutions in a way which will permit the parties to accept them as their own rather than as the mediator's ideas.

**The establishment of special boards.**   In simpler disputes one or more members of a mediating agency are usually assigned to the case, and representing the agency, use their good offices in an effort to settle the case. We have suggested that if the conflict is a particularly difficult one, a special mediatory or fact-finding board is frequently created.

These boards may be "all public" boards or they may be tripartite. In the former case it is expected that all members will be impartial. The membership of such boards is frequently established, however, in consultation with the parties in conflict. Occasionally certain members of such boards may be selected because they are known especially to have the confidence of the union and of management.

Tripartite boards impose a heavy mediating responsibility upon the chairman, who serves as the impartial member. They have the advantage, however, of bringing representatives or nominees of the parties into the center of the mediation effort. Such members can often be helpful in finding the way for the parties to retreat from extreme and untenable positions.

**Timing of the mediator's initial intervention.**   The time when the mediator enters a dispute may be of critical importance. In labor conflicts it has proved useful for the mediator to be aware of the dispute at its earliest stages so that his services may be offered before contending positions have become firm. He must enter the dispute at a time when strategic retreat can be gracefully executed. In most disputes the parties approach mediation with their own positions having been thoroughly discussed in their own circles. Any radical and hasty retreat from these carefully formulated positions is likely to have a substantial influence on the morale of the contending organization. The difficulties of mediation increase, therefore, in direct proportion to the embarrassment that attends concession. A face saved may be a dispute resolved.

On the other hand, it is recognized that if access to a mediator is made too easy, then much of the pressure of responsibility is removed from the parties at the bargaining table. If a mediator finds, upon entering a dispute, that there is evidence that the parties have not exhausted all possible resources of their own to bargain out a settlement, he should be free to send the case back to the parties for direct negotiation. This policy of turning back a dispute upon evidence of insufficient bargaining should be announced by the mediator as part of his working formula, and should also be accepted by the parties as part of the tradition of mediation. While few disputes are, in their entirety, turned back to the parties, certain points are often returned for negotiation.

The procedure of mediation in the United States has been to enter a dispute just previous to, or just following, the time when the parties have reached a deadlock. Government mediators have chosen this moment primarily because any further delay is likely to result in a strike, and any earlier entrance might unnecessarily interfere with the normal process of direct negotiation. It is also generally assumed that at this moment the parties will be most susceptible to mediation. The imminence of open conflict brings into focus a realization of its hardships and consequences. Negotiators are weary of argument, and their constituents are fearful of economic warfare and may be eager for a settlement. But as we have already suggested, there are many other factors which should be taken into consideration in judging the moment most suitable for a mediator to enter, and the combination and force of these factors will vary with each situation. Some of the most brilliant achievements of mediation have been possible only because an impasse was allowed to develop and continue to the point where both parties were so anxious for an exit from the deadlock that mediation was crowned with success.

Mediators are becoming more aware of the need for a considered judgment in timing their actions rather than automatically arriving just before the picket lines appear. In this they are aided by legislation. The Taft-Hartley Act gives the Federal Mediation Service the power to enter a dispute at any time it believes its services might be useful. A similar provision exists in the legislation establishing the New York State Mediation Board.

In 1948, out of the labor disputes coming before the New York State Mediation Board, the Board itself took the initiative in entering the dispute in 8 per cent of the cases. In 9 per cent of the cases the employer asked for the Board's intervention, and in 79 per cent of the cases the Board entered the case at the union's request. In 3 per cent of the cases the unions and the employer joined in requesting Board action.

Experience in the New York State Mediation Board indicates that the means through which the Board is brought into the case has at times been a very sensitive point. It is for this reason that in New York State there appears to be a rather widely accepted understanding between management and labor that if the intervention of the Mediation Board is to be requested by one or the other of them, the labor group will make the request. Because of

Federal and state mediation agencies have the freedom to offer their mediatory facilities on their own administrative motion at the time when they believe their services are likely to be most helpful.

sensitivity over this point, it has occasionally proved to be advisable for the Mediation Service to enter the dispute on its own initiative.

Theodore Kheel, formerly Commissioner of the New York City Division of Labor Relations, has commented on this point as follows:

It seems to me that mediation has to be initiated by someone other than the parties to a dispute. . . . But the way should be left open for either party to invoke mediation if it so desires. My experience in the Division of Labor Relations was that both management and labor were reluctant to assume the onus of invoking mediation because they felt that perhaps in that way they were showing some sign of weakness. As a result, we would try to protect the party that invoked mediation.[8]

The 30-day-notice provision has now somewhat diminished this problem as a serious one for the Federal Mediation Service.

The present generally accepted powers which state and Federal mediation services have to intervene in a dispute represent a great advance from the situation existing at the time the U.S. Department of Labor was first established in 1914. At that time, Secretary Wilson used with the greatest caution the powers given him to intervene and undertake mediation in labor disputes. Business groups in the country did not then look with favor on the Secretary's being given these powers because by implication it gave a recognition to trade unionism which industry in general was not prepared to grant. There has been since, however, the gradual recognition of the necessity of Federal and state mediation efforts. As a result, the Federal Service has made increasing use of its discretionary powers to intervene in disputes at an early stage and on its own initiative.

**Getting the parties together.** Mediation is an emotionally

[8]Letter of July 9, 1950, to Donald B. Straus.

charged process and, as Garfield and Whyte have pointed out, the mediator must see that these human emotions are constructively discharged, as well as deal with the substantive issues in dispute.[9]

On occasion, disputants may come to a mediator with emotions at such a high pitch that they are unwilling or unable to sit in the same room with one another. In such cases, the mediator's first role is to find an effective way of getting emotions cooled down. One proven technique is to get the parties together around less controversial subjects such as the procedure for the conduct of the mediation. The mediator may, during this period, have to act as messenger between the isolated groups.

**Building up of confidence: full expression of views.** During the initial period confidence and understanding between the mediator and the disagreeing parties must be built; a confidence both in the procedure and in the mediator. Each of the representatives of the parties must be given an opportunity to express his own views and the assurance that what he says has been understood. It is good practice, after each representative has spoken, for the mediator to express in his own words his understanding of what the representative has said. In doing this, he must exercise extreme caution not to give an idea of undue sympathy to the position of one party or the other. Any real or imagined bias will make the later tasks much more difficult.

Until each side has had an opportunity to present its position and has been assured that this position has been understood, the minds of the parties are pretty well closed to any sort of argument or suggestion. But after each side has had its say and has been understood, there is a disposition to give sympathetic under-

[9]Sidney Garfield and William Foote Whyte, "The Collective Bargaining Process: A Human Relation Analysis," *Human Organization*, Summer, 1950, published by the Society for Applied Anthropology, New York.

standing to subsequent discussion, often to quite an extraordinary degree.

While this procedure should be continued until everyone present has had an opportunity to unburden his mind, it must not be allowed to drag along until the parties begin to solidify their positions through repetition. Reiteration of points and arguments is the signal for a termination to this step in the procedure.

**Factual deflation.** The parties enter the discussion with their minds full of their own cause, the points of which have been talked out among representatives of their side, with the result that the points, both factually and in the argumentative sense, have become highly inflated.

Members of the War Labor Board in the Second World War often greeted factual disputes with the assertion that gentlemen cannot really disagree about a fact, they can only be ignorant about it. The mediator who is impartially trying to find out what the facts are and to reduce them to their true proportions and relations instinctively adopts a technique which tends to deflate inflated misunderstandings or misrepresentations of the facts. There is an accompanying deflation of the inflated arguments predicated on those misconceptions of the nature or relevancy of the facts.

Of course, the mediator, at this stage, can destroy the confidence which he has built up if in his treatment of the facts he shows partiality or impatience or lack of understanding. In the general run of cases, if the parties are meeting together, this step can be completed around the table, but it is sometimes useful to suspend the proceedings while prearranged and impartial examination of a particular fact or group of facts is undertaken.

**Raising doubts in the minds of the parties about positions already assumed.** As the exaggeration and misunderstanding is removed from the factual background of a dispute, the mediator can begin to raise doubts in the minds of both sides as to the justification of their respective positions. A willingness to abandon extreme positions is developed, followed by a movement from these previously assumed positions.

There is often in labor disputes, as in many other types of disputes, an honest inability to see the justice of the other party's case and a similar inability to see any limitations in one's own case. In some situations one party does not begin to think seriously about his position until faced with some action as drastic as a strike or lockout, and then the consideration may be complicated by emotional factors. In the great majority of cases, however, the parties, under the direction of a skilled mediator, can be brought to the point where they see the untenability of extreme positions which they may have adopted. This process can often be aided by the following techniques: (1) questioning one party about how he meets certain strong points in the position announced by the other party; (2) asking a party to reanalyze arguments previously presented but in the light of facts in their new proportion.

**Alternative solutions.**  At this stage, the mediator's sense of timing is most important. If he can make suggestions, not too soon or too abruptly, and if the parties will take up these suggestions for discussion, the mediator has made real progress. If he is premature in putting out a suggestion, he may destroy confidence in his impartiality. On the other hand, if he withholds the suggestion too long, he may miss a golden opportunity.

The mediator should keep in mind that during the negotiations each side will be sizing up the other, not only as to what appears to be its relative weighing of the issues involved, but also as to the manner in which it could be expected to carry out any agreement reached.

The mediator may find that party *A* wants something which *B* does not care particularly about and that *B* desires something very much which is relatively minor to *A*. If so, these issues might be disposed of and a certain "habit of agreement" established.

As the time approaches at which alternative solutions can be considered, it is important for the mediator to have made preliminary determinations of what would appear to be the reasonable expectations of the parties with regard to the principal items in dispute. It is likely that these "areas of reasonable expectation" intersect at some point. This intersection, if it can be ascertained correctly, becomes the point at which the initial agreement is likely to be reached.[10] The expectations of the parties to the dispute are determined not only by the various special pressures that have been brought to bear in the situation but even more fundamentally by the fluctuating tides of economic power. It is important, therefore, for the mediator to judge the basic economic and political trends into which this particular settlement will have to fit, for the object of the mediation effort is not so much to bring a settlement in line with what might be considered to be abstract justice as to effect a mutual adjustment of interest which, in the light of existing or developing circumstances, will be acceptable to the two parties to the dispute.

It may sometimes be effective at this point in the negotiations to deal with the parties separately in different rooms. This gives the mediator an opportunity to get each party to embrace the alternative solution as its own. There is danger that if the suggestion is made to both parties simultaneously, then one party might embrace it and the other feel impelled to oppose it. This is sometimes overcome in a very informal way around the conference table. It is extremely desirable not to spring an alternate solution upon the parties without advance warning so that they will not react adversely mainly because of its newness. It may also be

---

[10]From a paper, especially prepared for this study, by Arthur S. Meyer, former Chairman of the New York State Mediation Board.

necessary at this stage for the mediator to be prepared with some "face-saving" suggestions.

It is important for each party, during the negotiations, to come to understand the limitations within which the other party must work. This process may be facilitated by the mediator through his encouragement of the use of organizational or institutional terminology known to be familiar to the party having the greatest difficulty in understanding the other's point of view.

**Assessment of reserve powers possessed by mediator.** Up to this point, nothing has been said about reserve powers that may be available to the mediator, beyond his own power of persuasion and the general reasonableness of the parties. It is important that the mediator should evaluate his store of reserve powers, even though he should always be careful not to strain those powers beyond their capacity, and not to use powers that do not properly belong to him. As we have seen, mediators possess varying powers depending upon the machinery within which they are operating. Overstraining or abuse of powers may well bring the whole process of mediation into disrepute.

If either party is severely tempted to withdraw from mediation and to resort to a strike or a lockout, it may be useful to indicate afresh the likely consequences of such action. The parties thus approach a breakdown of negotiations with their eyes open and are reminded of the motives which brought them to mediation in the first place.

Not infrequently one of the parties would be willing to accept a compromise settlement were it not for outside political considerations. Management might be concerned with the effect of a certain clause upon other negotiations in which it has an interest. The union might be afraid that the best available deal would prove unpopular with the rank and file, or damaging in the light of the gains made by a rival organization. In such instances, but again with extreme caution, the mediator might explore possible ways of mitigating the wider repercussions of agreement or methods for removing the onus of an agreement from the party concerned and placing it upon his own shoulders.

In those instances where the public interest depends upon the continuity of work, there is a constant pressure of public opinion on both sides. Neither union nor management wants to be held responsible for a strike and the mediator may intimate to one group or the other, or possibly to both, that the unreasonableness of a position will not escape public attention. In cases of this kind, which deeply involve the public interest, there may be provisions of law which come into effect if the parties cannot agree and which may seem less unpalatable to one side or the other, or both, than the best available settlement to be gained in mediation. In extreme cases government seizure may be the alternative.

It is for the mediator, in assessing his reserve powers, to judge, in any particular case, the practical effect upon the disputants of the various types of action which might be taken. The milder of these are often recommended or instituted by the mediator or the mediating agency. As we have noted, in the event a breakdown in the mediation process appears imminent, other more forceful measures are frequently initiated by a separate government agency, or by the President. In these cases the mediator keeps in close touch with the other agency but usually does not himself assume responsibility for these supplementary actions.

One of the milder reserve powers of the mediator lies in his ability to influence some of the more intractable outside power factors which may have made settlement difficult.

**Cooling-off periods.** An atmosphere for fruitful negotiation may be difficult to establish if a strike is imminent or in progress. At times, tempers at the bargaining table may also become so strained that efforts to reach a settlement are severely handicapped. Under such circumstances it has sometimes been found useful to get the parties to agree to a "cooling-off" period, a time during which a strike, if imminent, is deferred. The theory is that if the parties could be persuaded to let production continue and the conditions of work remain *in status quo* for a short time, they might approach negotiation or mediation, freed from the tensions of a strike atmosphere, with emotions cooled and with a more constructive attitude.

An attempt was made to write this mediation tactic into the Taft-Hartley Act. The President is authorized to direct the Attorney General to seek an injunction (for a period of not more than 80 days) during which the *status quo* must be preserved and a strike is illegal. Since such an injunction may be sought only if a strike is harmful to the national interest, the major emphasis of this section is on maintaining production. The same statutory scheme also provides for a Board of Inquiry which is to issue two reports; one prior to the issuance of the injunction which is to inform the President of the nature of the dispute, and the other after the termination of the injunction reporting on any changes in the respective positions of the parties. While the injunction is in effect, the Federal Mediation and Conciliation Service is to continue its efforts to get agreement; otherwise there is no special provision for mediation.

Although the 80-day injunction is sometimes referred to as a cooling-off period, it has one unique and important characteristic —it is imposed upon the parties rather than being the product of their own volition. Then, too, it is of a predetermined duration, thus establishing a target date in the future when hostilities may be renewed under what appears to be statutory sanction. While the injunction is designed in the main to halt a disastrous strike, the Act anticipates that during the period of injunction efforts to reach voluntary settlement will continue. Experience, however, suggests that positions tend to harden and emotions heat up while the injunction is in effect. Not only is the "cooling-off period," because of its enforced character, a misnomer, but the usual experience is that when a dispute becomes sufficiently aggravated for a strike to be in prospect, emotions are not likely to cool down until some substantial progress is made toward dealing with the basic issues.

In those cases in which the parties can be persuaded through voluntary agreement to defer a strike for the purpose of providing a more conciliatory atmosphere in which to pursue settlement, the cooling-off period has, on the other hand, sometimes been found to be a useful device.

**Voluntary arbitration.** A mediator may find an opportunity to suggest that the parties submit their dispute to voluntary arbitration. The mere statement of this alternative is seldom sufficient. If presented at all, it should be accompanied by an attempt to get the parties to agree at least on the items they are willing to arbitrate, and to draw up a stipulation of the issues and criteria as guides to the arbitrator. This procedure would involve (1) the attempt to get agreement by the parties on such matters as the names of persons who would be acceptable as arbitrators; (2) an agreement upon the exact issue to be submitted to arbitration; (3) possible guides or criteria which the parties agree should be used by the arbitrator.

**Concluding the agreement.** After a basis of agreement has been established it is important that the mediator should keep at it until the understanding between the parties has been clearly expressed in a written memorandum. Otherwise, a possible agreement may fail through misunderstanding, accentuated perhaps by the not-quite-satisfied participants in the discussion. If that occurs, the mediator may lose all chance of ever getting an agreement.

# 2

## Mediation in Sweden

### BY CARL CHRISTIAN SCHMIDT

### Union-Management Organization in Sweden

The first Swedish trade unions were formed during the 1870's and 1880's. The beginnings were made in handicrafts, transportation, and industry. After various trade unions combined to form national unions, a number of these in turn combined in 1899 to form the Federation of Swedish Trade Unions (LO). This organization on the part of labor induced the employers to combine into organizations of their own, and some years after LO was founded the Swedish Employers' Association (SAF) came into being.

Laborers' groups have not been the only ones to organize. Over a period of years white-collar workers in private industry have organized their own interest groups. In 1931 several white-collar unions combined to form a central organization, which in 1944 also included in its ranks state and municipal employees. The name of Swedish Association of Professional Workers (TCO) was adopted. This organization is for the white-collar workers what the Federation of Swedish Trade Unions (LO) is for the laborers.

The right to strike has always been recognized in Sweden. Swedish punitive law contains provisions which prevent state and municipal employees from striking if they hold responsible positions or positions calling especially for independent action and responsibility in the performance of duties. These last-named categories, however, have formed their own "trade unions," which, although waiving the right to strike, authorize their representatives to negotiate in their interests. In actual practice, this does not prevent the organizations from notifying the government of intended resignations on the part of employee members. The usual time of such notification, given in advance, varies from three to six months. State and municipal employee organizations are, on the whole, of relatively recent origin.

Viewing the present system of collective bargaining from the point of view of the employee, it can be asserted that it is very homogeneously organized. The Swedish population is not characterized by any serious cleavages of race, language, or religion which conspire to prevent the growth of a unidirected labor movement. Nor have divisive political or social ideologies made themselves manifest. There is of course an independent syndicalist movement, but it numbers only 20,000 members and it is relatively insignificant. Those trade unions which are members of the LO are overwhelmingly oriented toward the Social Democratic party, while TCO and other central organizations are, in accordance with their bylaws, politically neutral. An important feature of the trade-union movement is that each trade union is not restricted to one locality but has the whole of Sweden in which to recruit members and to pursue its activities. This means that collective contracts can be drawn up which are valid for the whole country, provided only that the employers themselves are organized on a national scale.

Trade-union organizations are founded on a democratic base. Governing bodies and officials are elected by representative groups, called congresses, which meet every third or fifth year. Important questions, *e.g.*, notification of expiration of collective contracts or the drafting of new contracts, are decided by the individual votes of all trade-union members affected. The same procedure applies also to the calling of strikes. Governing bodies, however, do exercise certain rights of decision.

Employers' organizations are considerably more scattered. The Swedish Employers' Association (SAF) by and large represents industry, and its membership consists of those industries which, because of their nature, are in a position to carry through a lockout move. Regulations place greater power in the hands of the central organization than is the case within the trade-union movement, where LO lacks the power to direct the policies of member unions. Parallel organizations to SAF are to be found within the fields of retail trade, agriculture, shipping, commercial banks, insurance companies, hotels and restaurants, newspapers, and a number of handicrafts. Under the direction of SAF a certain measure of cooperation between these employer organizations does occur. In civil service occupations, Swedish cities, rural towns, and county governing bodies maintain their own "employer organizations." The state itself has set up a negotiating agency which represents it in its capacity as employer vis-à-vis employee groups working under the terms of collective contracts. Examples in point are the state-owned and -operated railway system, and the telephone and telegraph services.

### The General Legislative Background

As previously mentioned, LO and SAF are the main central organizations. Their relations have been decisive in determining the character of labor negotiations in Sweden. The strikes and lockouts which occurred just after the turn of the century focused the attention of the Riksdag and the administration on the question of solving and preventing similar conflicts in the future. LO and SAF, however, assumed an air of aloofness to any attempt from the state to meddle in their private concerns. When a law was proposed in 1903 concerning the mediation of labor disputes, it was rejected not only by industrial representatives but also by the LO. When in 1906 a new proposal was submitted, it was approved but won a bare majority in the First Chamber. In a similar manner, LO was a stout opponent of two 1928 laws on collective contracts and on a labor court. The former regulated collective contracts on the basis of existing practice, *i.e.*, it rationalized a *fait accompli*. The latter concerned the juridical settlement of disputes on the interpretation and application of collective contracts. When in 1935 the Riksdag added an amendment to the law, providing for seven-day notice of strikes and lockouts, LO opposed it just as violently. During the 1930's government authorities began discussing the concept of "protection of the neutral third party" in labor disputes and debating the issue of labor conflicts which might be detrimental to the public interest. SAF and LO both opposed further legislation. Both, however, found it to their interest to regulate these questions under the terms of the basic agreement (Saltsjöbaden Agreement) reached in 1938. The result of this has been to decrease the necessity of any intervention by state authorities, and the matter is no longer a subject of popular or political discussion.

The above shows that labor and management organizations

have exercised in the past, and can continue to exercise, all the necessary authority in connection with their activity without outside intervention. It is quite clear that the legislation on mediation, which aroused such opposition from both employer and employee organizations, nevertheless made a strong impression on the rank-and-file membership of these organizations. The first law on mediation passed in 1906 was very cautiously formulated. It placed no duties on the parties to a dispute, but contained rather a set of instructions for mediators on ways and means for them to proceed in disputes. In 1920 a law on mediation was passed which is still in force today. This law agrees in all main points with the 1906 law, except for subsequent amendments, *e.g.*, that in 1935 which defined the obligation of respective parties to give adequate notice in advance on strikes and lockouts.

The present law contains the following general provisions. The government is empowered to divide the country into several so-called "mediation districts." It appoints a mediator to cover each district. At the present time eight district mediators are in the field and concern themselves with labor-management disputes arising within their jurisdiction. Their appointment to office is of one year's duration. The government can at any time dismiss them and replace them with other persons, if the occasion so demands. Mediators receive a fixed annual salary. They are prohibited by law from accepting compensation from either of the disputants, in any form whatsoever. The duties of mediator constitute a parallel or subordinate activity which must be discharged in addition to those of a regular occupation. The ranks of district mediators include such varied occupational categories as judges, lawyers, and civil service employees. Other professional groups have also been represented at one time or another, *e.g.*, university teachers. District mediators operate under the supervision of the Royal Social Board, which has a special department called the Mediation Service for taking care of these matters.

Should a labor dispute affect the jurisdictions of two mediators, or perhaps the country as a whole, the affected parties notify the Mediation Service, which in its turn may recommend that one of the mediators assume the responsibility of attempting to get a settlement. The Royal Social Board may also suggest to the government the appointment of some other qualified person. Should the dispute be difficult of solution and important in its consequences, the government may appoint a commission of two to five qualified persons.

The antiquated nature of the present mediation law can only be explained in terms of the attitudes held by the respective "interest groups" at the turn of the century. According to the law, a mediator should summon the disputing parties to conference only if the conflict has led, or threatens to lead, to a strike or lockout of major importance. In actual practice, mediators regard themselves merely as consultants available at a moment's notice to parties who are unable to reach an agreement. It makes no difference whether the dispute affects many or few employees or whether the dispute concerns a possibility of impending strike or not. The law further prescribes that the mediators may not call the disputants to further negotiations if the disputants have already negotiated in the presence of the mediator and his services are considered unnecessary. This procedure is in accordance with the spirit of the old law, which did not wish to inflict any inconvenience upon the conflicting parties. Developments have shown, however, that on the whole mediators have not been overeager in their intervention. The present-day experience is that one or both parties voluntarily appeal for the expert services of the mediator.

Another old-fashioned legal regulation authorizes the mediator to propose arbitration if no agreement can otherwise be reached. The mediator, however, is forbidden by law to assume the offices of arbitrator. In Sweden, the "interest organizations" are opposed in principle to the use of arbitration in disputes on matters which they consider to be their exclusive interest, *e.g.*, settling hourly or piecework pay rates. It is, therefore, meaningless for a mediator to suggest a solution of the usual cut-and-dried collective contract disputes. This is in line with the careful distinction made between the functions of mediating and the functions of deciding, a distinction which the mediator is careful to observe and one which practice has confirmed as being normally correct. A mediator serving in the capacity of arbitrator of conflicting interests would be regarded as discriminating against the wishes of the party which has lost or feels that it is getting the worst of the deal.

The law still contains old-fashioned provisions concerning the methods of summoning the disputants before the mediator. These provisions are hardly important at the present time, however, since the spadework for negotiations takes place informally for the most part and without benefit of formal governmental intervention. The law generally prescribes procedures which are still followed today.[1]

The negotiations conducted by the conciliator with or between the parties to the dispute shall, in the first place, have the object of bringing about an agreement in accordance with the offers or proposals which may be made by the parties themselves in the course of the negotiations; if and in so far as it seems suitable for the purpose of bringing about a satisfactory settlement of the dispute, the conciliator shall urge acceptance of such adjustments and concessions as may seem reasonable for the purpose.

The law does not enumerate any special duties required of the conflicting interest groups. It is assumed the parties will be avail-

[1] Paragraph 6, Law on Mediation and Labor Disputes of May 28, 1920, as amended by the Law of September 11, 1936.

able when the mediator calls them to the conference table. For a long time no penalty was exacted of the party which failed to heed the summons. A 1936 amendment empowers the mediator to report the defaulting party to the Labor Court, which can re-issue the summons under penalty of fine. In this connection it can be mentioned that these fines have never been imposed. The interest organizations have established a tradition of appearing at the conference table when summoned. All parties are responsible for giving the mediator any vital information which he may request, with the reservation that all information be held in strict confidence.

### Present-day Mediation Practice

In present-day practice the attitude of the central organizations toward state intervention has remained the same as always, but the role of mediator has won ever greater acceptance since the mediation laws became effective. One of the most important reasons for this change in attitude is the fact that authoritative and capable persons have been appointed to serve as mediators. It is equally important that the law has been enforced not so much in the letter as in the spirit, and that it has given due heed to the wishes of the disputants in the appointment of mediators. As a matter of fact, developments have now reached the point where the government, if possible, sends a man who is in demand by both parties. Authorities have considered it a peace-promoting factor to send a person in whom both parties place the greatest confidence.

Collective contracts are at present of one year's duration, and in general call for three months' notice of expiration. In many cases the contracting parties may agree to shorten this period to one month or less. If the contract is to expire or if the notice of expiration is made shorter, the respective parties may judge the situation to be such that the services of an outside negotiator are considered necessary from the very beginning of the negotiations. According to law and attendant practice, the services of a mediator are not available before the parties themselves have attempted to reach agreement. In cases where law and existing practice do not prescribe the appointment of a state mediator, the parties usually summon a qualified person to serve as an impartial chairman during the negotiations. Experience has shown that the person functioning in these situations is almost always a mediator currently in office or one who has served previously as mediator. An impartial chairman acts in the strictest confidence of both parties and is entitled to remuneration from them for his services. Obviously, in such a capacity the mediator cannot perform in the same "steam-roller" fashion which characterizes his duties when he is publicly appointed. In this capacity he can hardly put forth proposals which do not meet with the favor of both factions. A glance at the contracts reached during the past year reveals that many agreements have been reached via the offices of an impartial chairman and thus the need for the use of the official mediation service was obviated.

In the event that negotiations reach an impasse, with or without the services of an impartial chairman, then the intervention of a public mediation agency is deemed necessary. If the disputes are local in nature and within the jurisdiction of one district mediator, a copy of a strike notice sent by the employees to the employers will serve to inform the mediator that his services are considered necessary. In other cases, where the trade union adopts less drastic methods, the mediator is requested by telephone or letter. Both parties often agree to call in the mediator to help in the continuation of negotiations. District mediators then can decide for themselves whether their good offices will actually serve to help the disputants reach an agreement. Should such possibilities exist, the mediator may summon both parties to the conference table.

If the conflict threatens to be of nation-wide scope, the disputants can set the negotiating machinery in motion, by the announced intention of workers to strike. In major disputes, developments seldom reach this advanced stage. Instead, one or both parties will inform the Mediation Service that its offices are considered desirable. If an impartial chairman already has been called to duty, this notification is usually made through him. Almost without exception, this chairman is then appointed to act as special mediator. If the matter requires the services of a mediating commission, the impartial chairman as a rule serves as head of this commission. The Mediation Service usually gives consideration to the wishes of disputants concerning the membership of these commissions. It is not an unusual phenomenon for the disputants to reach a private agreement concerning the selection of mediators, either individually or on commissions. If the parties agree, they usually then request the Mediation Service to secure the services of particular persons. Of course it is possible for tastes to differ, and in such an event the Mediation Service will recommend a person or persons who have not been proposed by either side.

Experience has shown that the disputants usually prefer a district mediator currently in office or one who has held the position before. The naming of an "outsider" generally encounters the objection from both sides that he lacks negotiation experience. This reaction does not derive so much from conservatism as from a realization that an inexperienced hand can do more damage than good at a conference table. This circumstance has substantially reduced the number of eligible mediators at times when several negotiations are under way simultaneously. The relative position of the mediator in the socioeconomic hierarchy is also of considerable weight in the final choice. The ideal combination, as experience has shown, is embodied in the man who is of high social standing and who has had negotiating experience.

This account has indicated that the average mediation commission consists of a chairman and between one and four members. In setting up these commissions, consideration is shown not only to the wishes of the disputants but also to those of the chairman and of the Royal Social Board in appointing persons who may yet be apprentices but who can be counted on to gain valuable experience in the field. During the 1920's the three-man commission was much used. It was sometimes composed of one chairman and two other members, enjoying, respectively, the confidence of employers' and employees' interests. Thus, the former president of LO represented labor, while the employers' spokesman was a bank director who had intimate connections with the larger industrial interests and their employer organizations. This system, which was known in the vernacular as "The Commission of Hostages," has not been used in later years, since it was obvious that the interest groups exacted far too many demands of the person who was supposed to promote their interests.

The system of mediation prevailing in Sweden has led to a condition in which a select few establish reputations as skillful negotiators, and as a result their services are in special demand. The difficulty of persuading the disputants to accept newcomers is considerable. On the other hand, a good man may incur the disfavor of one or both sides in a particular field, let us say breweries, and by degrees find himself on the outside looking in—a "has-been" as a mediator of brewery disputes. The experience of the recent past has shown, however, that certain trade organizations have come to rely regularly on the services of a particular mediating expert year after year. Such a mediator comes in time to acquire special familiarity with the problems of a certain branch or trade.

The foregoing account has largely concentrated on the dual function of the mediator as an impartial chairman and as an official mediator. Should the negotiations reach an impasse he can reappear in still another guise, namely, as chairman or member of a mediation commission. In this way, a process of negotiation by three stages is easily achieved. This step-by-step procedure is in itself not particularly desirable since it serves to protract matters to the disadvantage of both parties, who have been at times quick to proclaim their displeasure. Spontaneous strikes are one manifestation of this general dissatisfaction. The authorities have therefore consciously adopted a policy of recommending alternatives: either a mediating commission or a special mediator can be placed at the disposal of the parties. In the latter event, the disputants are made to consider, albeit unofficially, the mediator as the final alternative, and not to count on the selection of a commission if the negotiations fail to make progress. However, the step-by-step process is unavoidable in certain situations. The mediator quite often may judge the situation to be sufficiently serious to warrant the supporting action of a commission—which for both parties and the general public is an indication that matters have reached the last straw.

An essential factor is that the authority of the mediator, once he is chosen, is maintained throughout the entire negotiating procedure. This assures continuity of leadership. During the early years of collective bargaining, the initially appointed mediator occasionally did not last throughout the proceeding, and it was necessary to replace him with another. During the past 40 years, however, this circumstance has never occurred. Respect for the recommended mediator is an important consideration and it is in the interest of the parties concerned to maintain this attitude throughout the negotiations. If the negotiations have not proceeded to the satisfaction of the disputants, the likelihood is that another mediator will be appointed for the following year.

If the negotiations are prolonged, each party may, in the event a deadlock has been announced, give notification of strike or lockout. In recent years, however, they sometimes prefer not to give notification of strike but instead to prohibit performing all overtime work. Similar "notifications" can contrive to speed up negotiations, but they can also work in the opposite direction. A usual reaction is for the party which would be victimized by a strike threat to declare itself unwilling to undertake negotiations under duress. The negotiating situation is thus considerably complicated. Mediators, who are supposed to preserve the labor peace, usually appeal to the warning or notifying party to refrain from militant measures in view of the possibility of continued negotiations. Such a proposal made by the mediator is usually accepted without serious objections. The mediator as an impartial chairman obviously does not direct such an appeal to the notifying party in the event that delay would be detrimental to the latter's tactical position. As soon as possible, the mediator attempts to bring the disputants together for new negotiations.

If all mediation attempts prove futile, or open hostilities ensue, the duty of the mediator or the mediating commission is to "follow developments" and to call the parties to new negotiations as soon as it is felt that the situation warrants such a move. Even additional, extraneous causes may give rise to new mediation efforts, *e.g.*, a notification of the strike's spread (sympathy actions).

## The Development of Techniques

This account of mediation in Sweden has pointed to the desirability of mediators having "experience." Experience is somewhat difficult to define in this case, but the practice which has arisen in connection with Swedish negotiating procedure has given us a reasonable working definition. Each mediator has his own technique and his own methods of conducting negotiations, restricted only by his particular temperament and the circumstances involved. Certain general features are, however, common to all mediators in their way of negotiating. First of all their services are invoked *after* the disputants have attempted to reach an agreement by themselves. The results of preliminary efforts are always available in the form of previous collective contracts or appeals for amendments to these, as well as minutes kept of the proceedings. Statistical investigations, economic calculations, or other sources can also be made available and can be of inestimable value to the mediator, who makes it his business to acquaint himself beforehand with their details.

As a rule, negotiations in the presence of the government-appointed mediator begin with a meeting in which the delegates for all parties discuss the economic situation in general and cover the demands made by the respective parties only in outline form. After such a session the delegates usually retire to separate quarters, where they await developments. In the meantime, the mediator negotiates with the principal representatives for each side or, at the most, with committees consisting of two to three persons from each side. This form of negotiation is regarded as particularly significant because the mediator is in a position to achieve a more personal contact. Likewise, questions of a more delicate nature can be discussed more freely in the confines of a small room than in a large meeting hall. According to the situation, the mediator can negotiate with each side either on the smaller or on the larger scale. As a rule it is the task of the organization chairmen, or a smaller committee, to make progress reports to their delegations. At the same time the chairmen keep in constant touch with their delegations in order to get information which may be needed by the mediator.

Mediators confine themselves to those questions upon which the disputants have failed to agree at their preliminary discussions. As soon as possible, a mediator attempts to work out a compromise proposal which is in the nature of a "feeler" or rough draft, which may embrace the whole scope of the problem situation or perhaps only a certain part of it. The mediator does not commit himself at this stage by drawing up a formal document to which he affixes his signature, but merely submits a rough draft which can be freely discussed by the affected parties. The first draft may encounter strong objections from one or both sides and a revision is often necessary. Several drafts may have to be submitted before the mediator arrives at a considered judgment of what will be the correct proposal. The final draft is then written in detail, signed by the mediator, and then submitted to the parties for their examination and preliminary approval. By preliminary approval is meant that the delegates for both sides commit themselves to work towards the final, definite approval on the part of the member organizations affected. Should one or both sides refuse to sign, the mediator usually withdraws his proposal and declares that it is to be regarded as never having existed. As a rule, this move is a signal for declaring an impasse in the negotiations. However, on certain occasions new proposals may be made which in their final documentary form will win the approval of both parties. In exceptional cases, the mediator may submit a "take-it-or-leave-it" proposal over the heads of the disputants to the rank-and-file membership, without asking the delegates for their preliminary approval. This drastic step is hardly necessary except in cases where considerations of the public interest call for the public submission of a mediation proposal, or where the chief delegates intimate to the mediator that the proposal will eventually be accepted even without preliminary approval.

A mediation proposal can be approved by the employer delegation already at the conference table. However, on the opposite side the proposal must be submitted to the affected laborers for their approval by individual vote, or to a chosen group of labor representatives meeting at so-called contract conferences. Trade-union bylaws generally stipulate that a qualified majority of the members concerned must agree on whether or not a strike is to take place. According to this regulation, the trade-union leadership is empowered to approve a mediation proposal even if the majority opposes it, provided that a majority in favor of striking has not been attained.

The foregoing account of Swedish mediation has shown the desirability of the parties themselves reaching agreement without state intervention. They assume full responsibility for the collective bargaining procedure, which will differ according to the type of business involved. State intervention is confined to a few laws which are of compulsory nature. Under this heading come the legal regulation of collective contracts, laws on the settlement of disputes concerning the interpretation and application of collective contracts, laws on the rights of association and negotiation, together with obligation to notify affected parties and mediators of intended strikes and lockouts. The state has provided for the appointment of eight district mediators who are available when needed, and in major disputes furnishes special mediators and commissions. No compulsion is placed on the parties other than the obvious pressure to which the negotiating system compels them. It has happened, and still does happen, that the government or individual cabinet ministers, after due consultation with the mediator or commission concerned, summon representatives of the disputing parties in order to give them a "gentle reminder" that the welfare of the nation depends upon a peaceful settlement of their disputes. In a few cases in which the public interest was affected, the subject of a special coercive law came up for discussion in legislative committees. Such a law was seriously debated, for example, in connection with the threatened strike of registered nurses in 1951. Compulsory measures have, however, always been avoided in view of the fact that disputants have reached agreements, even if they came in the eleventh hour. Because of this, Sweden is perhaps the only country in the world today in which interest organizations have been able to maintain a relatively unlimited freedom.

Finally, it should be pointed out that district mediators, as well as special mediators and mediation commissions, must pursue their assignments independently once they have been appointed to them. They do not act in accordance with directives from the government or from the Royal Social Board on the contents of an agreement or concerning the methods to be used in the negotiating process. Together with the affected parties, they must judge to what extent, and when, a mediation proposal should be submitted, or whether or not the negotiations have reached a standstill. Likewise they must decide whether renewed negotiations, perhaps reinforced by additional mediating personnel, are desirable or worth while. The various mediating missions willingly maintain contact with their home offices in Stockholm to keep them informed of the progress which is being made in the more important negotiating situations. In the same way that the interest organizations are completely free to act and to make at the conference table those decisions for which they are responsible, so the mediating agencies have considerable freedom in performing the responsibilities and duties assigned to them.

# 3

## The Settlement of Labor Disputes
## in Great Britain

### BY SIR FREDERICK W. LEGGETT

### The Development of Conciliation Machinery

In the latter part of the eighteenth century and the beginning
of the nineteenth, Parliament in Great Britain was engaged in
sweeping away the Tudor Code, under which public authorities
entered largely into the regulation of workers' conditions, and
in preparing the way for a policy of *laissez faire*. It is interesting
to follow from that time the gradual working out of the relationship of state to industry and the development of constitutional
relations between the employers and workers. In the new factories there was an almost complete dominance of employers

over workers, and the conditions of child workers led to the passing of the Hours and Morals of Apprentices Act, 1802. In later acts protection was extended to all children in textile mills, and this was followed by the protection of women workers. It is typical of methods in Great Britain to commence with experimental legislation and to extend that legislation to wider fields when it has been found to be practicable. Thus all the Factory Acts up to 1833 were confined to textile mills. Further extensions were made until in 1878 practically all industries were covered and at the present time there is a wide code of health and safety measures in operation.

The wage rate, however, is the all-important factor in the relations between employer and employee because this is the chief factor in the determination of the standard of life and the basis on which workers compare their own position with that of others. With the repeal in 1824 of the acts which made combinations illegal, the trade unions, which had been operating secretly, were able to come into the open, and although for a time workers were absorbed in political issues such as corn-law reform, factory legislation, and the struggle for a wider enfranchisement, our history from 1850 onward is one largely of the growth of the power of trade unions in the field of industrial regulation. The cotton industry, which first passed over to the factory system, led the way to nineteenth-century trade unionism, but it was the Amalgamated Society of Engineers in 1851 which first established the model of centralized expert administration of the various branches of a trade union throughout the country. It was the leaders of this union, in association with those of the Carpenters' and Joiners' Union, the Bricklayers' Union, the Iron Founders' Union, and the Boot and Shoe Workers' Trade Union, who fought for the legal recognition of trade unions which was given in the laws of 1871 and 1875.

The agreements made were generally with individual employers or with a local group of employers. Local Joint Conciliation Boards were also established for the purpose of providing standing voluntary machinery for settling disputes. While these Boards showed differences in detail they were of a uniform general type. The essential feature was that trade difficulties, in the first instance, should be discussed by those best qualified—the employers and workers concerned. Each party to the dispute had equal representation. In the event of failure to agree, the matter was referred to referees or an arbitrator chosen according to some agreed plan. These arrangements were for the most part short-lived, but there are one or two notable exceptions in which the Boards still operate successfully. In the iron and steel trade, for example, in which there has been no stoppage of work of any importance for over 50 years, this system has been in operation for over 80 years. A special feature in this case is that, if the discussions in a particular works fail, the matter is referred to a Board of employers' and workers' representatives in the same locality. While not concerned themselves in the disputed matter, these Boards know the conditions of the trade in other works and the traditions and customs of the trade. If there is failure to agree on a finding, the matter is referred to arbitration. Another feature of the industrial relations in this industry is that no publicity is given to discussions and differences.

The modern system of collective negotiations over a wider area was begun during a lockout of engineers in 1852 when all district branches joined together to support those in the area concerned. Since that time national organizations on the part of both management and labor have developed generally in industries. While the early trade unions were confined to particular crafts in which there was a natural binding force derived from a mutual desire to protect the conditions and scope of each craft, the large-scale organization of general workers began with the successful strikes of dock workers and gas workers in 1880. At the present time the two largest unions are ones which accept members from any industry and from any occupation. One of them, the Transport and General Workers' Union, is divided into sections according to industries and operates in practice as a federation of unions. These unions have had great success and influence, and a powerful position, industrially and politically, has been given to their leaders by their large membership. There is a substantial body of opinion, however, which holds that, as their members have only the nexus of being workers and do not have the fellowship of being in the same craft or occupation, the effect of their growth will be to weaken trade unions as industrial bodies and, in the end, to damage trade unionism. In some industries the craft unions have extended their scope to cover all workers in those industries and there is a constant state of friction between craft and other unions. This friction has been increased by the fact that the earnings of workers regarded as unskilled or semiskilled have come nearer the level of those of highly skilled workers.

The first great movement toward this position took place in the First World War as a result of equal periodical advances being given in arbitration awards to all classes of workers. In view of the fact that, as a result of political action, all workers receive considerable benefits in kind in the form of free education, rent and food subsidies, and similiar social security benefits for the same contributions, the standard of life is no longer determined only by individual earnings. This fact is bound in due course to have its effect on industrial organization. This, however, is a subject of speculation and, as this chapter is concerned only with the machinery for the settlement of disputes, it need only be said that the social advances brought about by political action have produced an entirely different situation from that in which trade unions were formed and in which they grew to their present magnitude. Trade unionism commenced as an industrial and not a political movement and the disputes were between employers and their employees. Today the government tends to be a party in disputes and becomes more quickly involved.

### Early Attempts at Arbitration

From the beginning of the nineteenth century there have been recurring attempts to find a short way to the settlement of industrial disputes by compulsory arbitration, with penalties for refusal to observe arbitration decisions. Except under war conditions in which the state becomes the chief source of payments and the chief buyer, these attempts have always completely failed. Against the resistance of large bodies of workers, there is no real power to make compulsion effective. After an Act of 1747 which gave justices of the peace jurisdiction over disputes between employers and workers during the period of a hiring, both sides in the cotton industry petitioned for a bill to give them the right to demand arbitration. The country had been at war with France since 1793, and in 1800, when the petitions were presented, the employers found themselves unable to regulate wages and the operatives were unable to protect themselves against arbitrary reductions. An Act was passed under which each side was empowered to appoint an arbitrator and the award of such arbitrators was to be final and binding. Should the arbitrators fail to agree the difference was to be submitted to a justice of the peace who had to give a decision within the space of three days.

It is of interest that this early law gave to the arbitrators power to summon witnesses and to examine on oath. Almost at once another Act was passed extending these provisions to all trades and industries, but this Act contained also a code of provisions against what were termed unlawful combinations of workmen for raising wages. These Acts were not successful as the power given to each side to nominate arbitrators caused great inconvenience and delay. In 1804, therefore, the Acts were amended by providing a new procedure whereby, if the parties to the difference agreed to abide by the decision of a justice of the peace, he might decide it but, if not, he was to nominate a panel of four or six persons—one-half employers and one-half operatives—and from this panel the parties were to choose one person each to act as arbitrators. If the two arbitrators failed to agree, the justice of the peace was to decide. The payment of £10 by the defaulting party to the other was the sanction for the performance of the award.

This provision again was the subject of complaint. The principle of the Act was condemned by the exponents of the fashionable political economy of that day, and in 1824 a new Act introduced a system of referring disputes to referees appointed by a justice of the peace or finally to a justice of the peace. There was an important limitation—that future rates of wages could not be fixed "unless with the mutual consent of both master and workman." Either party could demand arbitration.

This Act was amended in 1827 but it had not proved satisfactory, and it and the principle of compulsory arbitration received their quietus when, in 1838, a mechanic at Kelso was convicted under the Act and sent to jail on the complaint of his employer. There was much agitation among workers and although the Act was amended in one or two details, it was impossible to restore the confidence of the workers in legislation which contained the sanction of imprisonment. From then onward attention was directed to methods of voluntary conciliation and arbitration. In 1859 a bill was introduced to establish Courts of Conciliation and a system of voluntary arbitration, but the bill was not passed.

In 1867, after seven years of work by Lord St. Leonards, and with the good will of both employers and workers, an Act was passed which authorized employers and workers in any trade or occupation to form themselves into Councils of Conciliation on obtaining a license from the Crown, each Council to consist of not less than two employers and two workers and a chairman. The awards might be enforced in the same way as those under the Act of 1824, that is, by distress, sale, or imprisonment. No Council was ever set up and the Act became a dead letter. It seems, however, to have been the basis of a statute of the State of New York in 1886, but only a very few boards were appointed under it. In 1869 a Committee of Trade Unions recommended the establishment of a Court of Arbitration which should be voluntary, and in 1872 an Act was passed to carry this out. The Act enabled the contracting parties to bind themselves to settle every class of dispute by arbitration. Its intention was to extend the Act of 1824 in such a way as to obtain a different form of tribunal and to enforce the decisions arrived at. It was never put into force and only provided further evidence that, whatever the form of tribunal, arbitration and the enforcement of awards were not acceptable or practicable ways of avoiding or settling industrial disputes.

There were various reasons for the failure of all this legislation, but the main reason was that the parties were not prepared to accept the severe penalties for nonobservance. It does not appear to have occurred to anyone that the awards of tribunals should have only the same validity as an agreement between the parties, which is the basis on which arbitration awards have been observed in more recent times with exceedingly rare exceptions.

### Mediatory Intervention by the State

**The Conciliation Act of 1896.** In and prior to 1891 there had again taken place a series of strikes and lockouts, and attention was called to state action as a means of prevention or settlement of labor disputes. A Royal Commission was appointed in 1891 to inquire into various questions affecting the relations between employers and workers and to report whether legislation could, with advantage, be directed to the remedy of any faults that might be disclosed. As a result of their recommendations the Conciliation Act of 1896 was passed. This Act conferred statutory authority on the Board of Trade (which was subsequently transferred to the Ministry of Labour when it was established in 1916) to intervene in an industrial dispute. The Act was framed on a purely voluntary basis and enabled the Board of Trade:

1. To take such action as seemed expedient to promote an amicable settlement of a difference.
2. On the request of either party interested to appoint a conciliator to assist in securing a settlement.
3. To appoint an arbitrator to determine a difference with the consent of both parties thereto.

This Act enabled the government to do very little that it was not previously empowered to do, but its great advantage was that it gave a particular government department a definite duty toward, and relationship with, the movement in the direction of the peaceful settlement of industrial disputes. The Board of Trade could inquire into the causes and circumstances of any existing or apprehended difficulty, and, on the application of either or both parties, take action as described above. Under the fostering care of Sir George (later Lord) Askwith, the Act became an important means of settling industrial differences.

Judged by later experience the number of cases dealt with was small. In 1898, 12 cases were dealt with; in 1899, 11 cases. The greatest number in any year was 99 in 1913. The important consequence of the Act was that under it a corner of a government department became interested in and concerned with industrial disputes as a matter of official duty and the art of conciliation and arbitration began to develop. It became someone's job to take a hand, from an impartial standpoint and with the authority of the government behind him, in a dispute which was involving loss and public inconvenience. The public gradually became not only accustomed to intervention but also expectant of it.

The years before the First World War were years of industrial unrest in which serious national strikes occurred. Settlements were largely reached through the good offices of the Board of Trade. These years of work before the war proved that strikes and lockouts could be adjusted and provided a general experience which made possible the system of conciliation and arbitration adopted and adhered to during the war.

During the war the state assumed a large measure of responsibility for both production and consumption, and the individual rights of both employers and workers were curtailed. By agreement between the government, the employers' organizations, and the trade unions, wages were largely fixed either by departmental orders or by arbitration. Strikes and lockouts were made illegal on munitions work unless, within a period of three weeks from the time a dispute was reported, the Board of Trade had not either settled the dispute or referred it to arbitration.

For the purpose of the present chapter it is necessary to refer only to one result of this controlled system. While the membership and potential authority of the trade unions greatly increased, collective bargaining was practically suspended. Workers suffered from the disparity between wages and rising prices, from housing difficulties, and from the many other grievances arising from war conditions. They saw their officials tied by agreements which fettered their liberty to take strong action. In addition the officials were largely occupied in activities connected with state machinery. This caused a certain neglect of day-to-day troubles in the workshops and left the way open to unofficial leaders not bound by agreements. A substantial shop steward movement developed which led to serious stoppages of work and constituted a grave threat to the production of munitions.

The simple fact is that members of trade unions pay their contributions for the purpose of securing wholehearted action in their interests, and they lose confidence in their leaders if they appear, by making agreements either with the government or with employers, to fetter their own freedom to take strong action on behalf of their trade-union members. As will be seen below, the lesson learned in this respect in the First World War was applied in the Second World War with the result that, although the period of the war was much longer, the government was never threatened with a breakdown of authority. Nor were wages raised to the same uneconomic level in relation to normal conditions. This situation arose in 1914–1918 from the early failure of an attempt by the government to keep wages stationary and the forced substitution of a policy of regular awards at short intervals by a standing arbitration tribunal called the Committee on Production. Soon after the end of the war there were serious stoppages of work in several great industries, arising from the substantial reductions of wages which became necessary. These were mostly settled by conciliation but, in one or two cases, only the exhaustion of the capacity to fight brought the disputes to an end.

**The preference for voluntary arrangements.** Arising from the experience of the war and the reports of the Whitley Committee, which had been appointed toward the end of the war to examine the means of improving the relations between employers and employed, the machinery of government and of industry entered on a period of progressive enlargement. In the political field labor had emerged as a new party which exercised a growing influence on national policy, especially in the field of social legislation.

In recognition of the claims of organized workers for a higher status in industry the Committee recommended that in industries in which both sides were well organized a Joint Industrial Council should be set up. These Councils were to have as their object the regular consideration of matters affecting the progress and well-being of the industry from the point of view of all engaged in it in so far as this was consistent with the general interest of the community. One important object of this, besides bringing workers' representatives into a position of greater responsibility in the general affairs of an industry, was to encourage regular meetings instead of meetings only when differences had arisen. While about 60 Joint Councils were set up a large proportion came to an end within a comparatively short period. With few exceptions, those which have remained active have concerned themselves mainly with wages and working conditions.

In many of the principal industries such as engineering, shipbuilding, and cotton, where there was already agreed machinery for negotiations, it was preferred to make no change. Moreover, these industries were not prepared to adopt any standing agreed arrangements for the reference of disputes to arbitration. The general principles of their joint machinery were that, in the first place, a difference should be discussed within the place of work and then, in some cases, with the local trade-union official. Failing settlement it would be discussed between the trade union and the employers' association locally. Finally it would be discussed, if necessary, between the national organizations on both sides, leaving them always free to agree, if they wished, to refer the matter to arbitration if no settlement was reached between them. There is still a strongly held view that, when final disagreement may lead to a serious stoppage of work, there is a maximum sense of responsibility on both sides to try and find a basis of agreement. It is felt that, without this fear of work stoppage, or if there is a certainty that arbitration can follow, there is no such reality in the negotiations and no such disposition to make concessions. In other words, the parties will order their action in such a way as to leave themselves in the best position at the final stage, when a third party will be involved.

As regards the general policy of the government for the settlement of industrial disputes the Whitley Committee recommended that arbitration should not be compulsory but by the voluntary agreement of the parties. They recommended, however, that a standing permanent arbitration tribunal should be set up, leaving parties free to have any other form of tribunal if they so desired. The Committee also recommended that the government should use legislative power to set up, at its discretion, an inquiry into the causes and circumstances of a dispute. Courts of Inquiry could be appointed, which could, if they so desired, take evidence on oath and require documents to be produced. Such a Court could reach findings but these would have no binding force on the parties. The main object was to inform the public of the facts relating to disputes which seriously affected the public interests.

These recommendations were implemented in the Industrial Courts Act of 1919, the standing tribunal being called the Industrial Court. This had a permanent president with a panel of chairmen in case it was desired to have more than one hearing at a time. There are permanent employers' and workers' representatives and panels of such representatives who can be called in when required. While this Court has always been used to a fairly large extent, parties to disputes have preferred in the majority of cases to have either a single arbitrator or a board, with joint agreement on the personnel to be used.

It had been hoped by those who favored the idea of a permanent tribunal that both sides in industry would like a system which would permit the building up of a code of decisions and general principles and which would coordinate arbitration awards. These hopes have been completely disappointed. Those in a particular industry wish always to have the assurance that only the facts in their industry will be considered, and they do not wish their own differences to be determined by reference to a decision taken in another industry by the same tribunal. There is always the chance that another tribunal will give a more favorable award and, in any case, arbitration is not attractive as a means of settling a dispute if the result can already be seen by the party which is making the claim. Thus, as in other fields, a theoretical advantage has been nullified by the facts relating to human nature. The Industrial Court has never become more than one of many forms of tribunal and has never reached the status intended for it.

**Governmental fact finding: Courts of Inquiry.**    Courts of Inquiry, when properly timed and not too often used, have proved to be of great value in preventing disputes or facilitating their settlement. They are usually constituted of an independent chairman, who may be a judge or a person of similar standing in regard to character and impartiality, and representatives of employers and workers, not connected with the industry in which the dispute has arisen. As the Court has no power to give decisions binding on the parties there is no difficulty in obtaining all relevant evidence. The hearing itself is not only valuable for the full information which it provides, but it also serves a useful purpose in causing the parties to state their case in an atmosphere removed from partisanship and bad feeling.

A Court of Inquiry is not, and must not be, used as a form of arbitration, because in that case the parties would be placed in a false position and would not be ready to be as frank as is desirable. The findings, however, have often been of great value. Such findings have frequently been the basis on which negotiations have been resumed. They have often supplied the foundation for a settlement. It is important that there shall be no certainty that a Court of Inquiry will be appointed if other means of settlement have failed. If there were such certainty, the tactics of one or other party would be ordered accordingly, and Courts of Inquiry would lose their value.

**Regional conciliation machinery.** In addition to the new statutory provisions of the Industrial Courts Act, the Ministry of Labour widened its organization by placing conciliation officers in different parts of the country, centered in Birmingham, Manchester, Leeds, Newcastle, Glasgow, and Cardiff, in addition to those in London from which alone the Board of Trade had operated in the prewar years. This was for the purpose of pursuing a constructive policy for the prevention of disputes rather than confining action to intervention in disputes when they occurred. It was the business of these officers to keep in close but unobtrusive touch with representatives of the industries in their areas and, by their personal relationships, to become persons with whom such representatives could usefully, and in confidence, discuss their difficulties. In all possible circumstances they endeavored to secure the establishment of joint machinery through which industries or individual undertakings could have a means of settling the differences that might arise. Much of their work was educative and slowly but surely, over the years, the habit of discussion rather than fighting was inculcated.

The conciliation officers, who were all carefully chosen, had as their great asset the fact that all confidences were carefully kept and that, while keeping this confidence, they were able, with the knowledge at their disposal, to guide the representatives on both sides towards a way of settlement. It has always to be remembered that, while strikes receive great publicity, the main business of industry is carried on by innumerable agreements daily and it was the task of the conciliation staff to see that both the means for these, and their number, were as great as possible.

### Recent Experience in Conciliation and Nonenforceable Arbitration

Looking at the whole position it is clear that conciliation is overwhelmingly the factor through which peaceful settlements are reached in industry. While arbitration awards may be accepted as a settlement, they come to people whose minds are in opposition and are, in fact, only acceptable as the least of evils in the circumstances. They frequently leave a feeling of hostility. Conciliation discussions may go on for many hours, or for many days, but the effect is to bring minds away from their first position to an understanding of the facts on both sides and to a final feeling that each side has been able to have its point of view taken into full consideration in reaching agreement. This is of first importance when each side starts by being so fully convinced of the strength of its case and of the unreasonableness of all who are opposed to it. Moreover, such discussions under skillful and experienced guidance leave a relationship which is likely to be more lasting and fruitful than that produced by a decision of a third party. It has also been shown that, as conciliation officers accumulate a record of successes, they acquire an authority which gives a confidence to the parties to a dispute that their intervention is most likely to result in a settlement.

It has been the invariable object of conciliators not only to settle a particular dispute but to make the agreement a basis for machinery which will prevent others. Of the many cases which could be cited it may be of interest to refer to the dispute affecting the whole of the cotton industry in 1932. Intervention was deliberately postponed by the writing of letters until the strike had been in operation for some days. Even when action was taken under public pressure it was still too early, having regard to the hard state of mind of those involved. The conciliator, therefore, in order to gain time and in order also to let the two sides have the experience of agreeing to something after a long series of disagreements, occupied four days in getting agreement on new permanent conciliation machinery and on the principles for the observance of collective agreements. As neither of these matters touched the wages and other matters which had caused the dispute, there was naturally some criticism, but the main object had been gained and the parties, in long and extended meetings, applied their now recognized ability to agree to reaching a settlement on all issues. It is important to note that this approach could only be made with confidence by the conciliator on the basis of an intimate knowledge of the facts and personalities of the industry, and on the basis of a sufficient trust by the parties in the conciliator's experience to make them feel that there was method in his apparent madness.

There has been no dispute of any importance in this industry since that time, and it is of interest to see the features of the conciliation machinery which have produced this result. It was agreed that the industry should appoint, by agreement between the two sides, an independent chairman, and that each side should appoint a representative not connected with the cotton industry. These three were to act as a standing Conciliation Committee to sit with the two sides in case of a deadlock. Failing agreement the chairman was bound to make recommendations, but these were not binding on the parties. A binding decision could only be made on the joint *ad hoc* request of the two sides.

This procedure brought the experience of other industries to minds obsessed by their own industry's traditions. It also recognized in addition the outstanding fact that, as a rule, there is an objection to being bound by a third-party decision, but that if there is freedom to accept or reject such a decision it will probably be accepted. There is everywhere a deep desire to preserve sovereignty and freedom of choice to the last.

In the interwar years there have been many disputes, including a general strike in sympathy with the coal miners. This was a period in which depression brought hardships of a type to leave indelible impressions on the minds of all who experienced unemployment and even on the minds of their children. These memories are likely to remain for some time a disturbing factor in industrial relations. It can be said, however, that the general system of collective agreements, supplemented by conciliation and arbitration, warded off the worst consequences. Together with social security and other legislation, they maintained stability. The result was that, when the Second World War came, the government, as a deliberate act of policy, was able to leave to the collective machinery of industry the control of wages. In agreement with both sides of industry steps were taken to control those factors, such as the price of necessities, which make wage claims inevitable and, on their side, the employers and trade unions were regarded as trustees for the safeguarding of the national economy.

Throughout the war collective machinery was in full operation with the result that there was no repetition of the unofficial movement which had caused so much trouble in the earlier war. By agreement with both sides, disputes were made illegal unless the Minister of Labour had not settled them or referred them to arbitration within three weeks from the date of being reported. A special tribunal, the National Arbitration Tribunal, was set up but disputes could still be dealt with by other tribunals. There was no regular review of wages as in the First World War and, while wages increased, the restraint shown by trade unions was evidenced by the longer interval between claims. Government action in the interests of the workers was much concerned with welfare measures.

While the above policy indicates an advance in industrial organization and joint machinery, it also shows that the government recognized that, if employers and workers were not prepared to assume a large measure of responsibility for keeping demands within reasonable limits and for the avoidance of stoppages of work, there was no power that the government could use to enforce these conditions. In fact, while the general position was satisfactory, there were disputes and stoppages in cases where advantage could be taken of favorable circumstances. The very fact that restraint is being exercised by a majority makes it easier for less responsible or less unselfish people to cause trouble. As we noted in the case of the mechanic of Kelso, one attempt to punish workers for striking illegally indicated that this power could not be enforced when a substantial number of workers were involved. Proceedings were taken against 1000 miners, and the Court imprisoned three trade-union officials and imposed a fine of £1 on each of the men. Only nine paid the fine and it was obvious that, if further proceedings were taken, this refusal would continue, and that there would be no alternative but to send the men to prison. It was clear that such action, apart altogether from the limitation of prison space, would be likely to cause a wider stoppage of work and could not be taken. The Minister of Mines, on whose authority the first proceedings had been conducted, settled the dispute by conciliation and himself asked for the release of three officials who had been imprisoned and for the cancellation of the fines on the men. This action was taken.

The long period of the war and the general satisfaction with the National Arbitration Tribunal and its awards created a disposition toward arbitration which has continued since the war ended. In fact, the active experience of a large number of present trade-union leaders has been confined to a period of rising wages and conditions and to the comparatively easy course of arbitration. The position is likely to change if less favorable circumstances bring adverse awards. In such circumstances trade union strength and negotiating capacity would again become the important factors, and there would be resistance to settlement by arbitration if it was considered that a fight would produce a more favorable result. Each generation produces new causes of discontent and only workers who lived in harder times realize how great has been the improvement of wages and conditions in this generation. The general reluctance to suffer any reduction, however, would not be lessened by this fact because present-day workers are conscious only of their own experience.

Over the past 15 years, including the war period, there has been so much political action for the improvement of social conditions and so much ministerial intervention in industrial troubles, that it seems probable that the government will be more deeply involved in future industrial strife than in past times of peace. It will be more difficult to avoid the undesirable results which come from the direct opposition of government and workers. This is a matter of speculation. It is to be noted that social security measures, school meals and child allowances, and the refund of income tax when a reduction of income is caused by a work stoppage, have created circumstances in which workers do not quickly feel hardship as the result of a strike. This being so, the preservation of order in a democracy depends much more than ever before on a personal sense of responsibility, and it is toward the creation of this that educational and other efforts have to be directed.

In Great Britain, as elsewhere, there are different stages of maturity in the orderly regulation of various industries which may be described as different stages in industrial civilization. The capacity to apply constitutional and peaceful measures varies according to these conditions and, as human beings remain little changed, much time must elapse before fighting ceases to be an early result of disputes.

The distrust of compulsory arbitration with government enforcement has been shown by the recent agreement of organized employers and workers to the modification of the War Order on this subject. The new Order provides that disputes may be reported to the Minister under the Order and, if he is satisfied that any agreed joint machinery in the industry concerned has been fully used, he must refer the dispute within 14 days to the Industrial Disputes Tribunal which has taken the place of the National Arbitration Tribunal. An award of this Tribunal becomes part of the terms of contract between the employers and workers concerned. There is no other penalty for nonobservance. In order to prevent unofficial leaders and groups of workers from using this procedure, disputes can be reported under this Order only by employers' organizations or trade unions which habitually take part in the voluntary settlement of terms and conditions of employment through joint machinery, or which, in the absence of such joint machinery, represent a substantial proportion of employers or workers in the trade or industry, or section of trade or industry concerned. This provision indicates the reality of the fear of giving any chance to unofficial leaders to act on behalf of a group of workers and so weakening the constitutional machinery by which members of the trade unions are bound.

It is to be noted that this Order is additional to the Conciliation Act and the Industrial Courts Act which are still fully operative. Employers and trade unions, therefore, are not bound to seek arbitration only under the Order or to have awards subject to any other than voluntary observance. Under whatever law arbitration is sought, a dispute cannot be referred to arbitration by the Minister unless it is quite clear that all agreed joint machinery has been exhausted.

There is no finality in human relationships, either in association in work or in other circumstances. The main objective must be to take all possible action to see that the disposition to fight is exercised in the least harmful ways and to secure the peaceful discussion of matters which would otherwise involve great loss and damage. There must be a continuous use of all experience in avoiding ineffectual courses and a constant adaptation of industrial machinery to meet changing needs and conditions. It is mainly by conciliatory methods that men and women can be assisted to act with a sense of responsibility and good will toward those with whom they are associated. It will, unfortunately, remain the case that they will only be driven to serious thought by some suffering of the results of foolish action. The timing of outside action must always be a decisive factor in regard to possible success. It is also always necessary to act on the basis that each disputant is convinced of the rightness of his case and to realize that there can be no easy way to convince him that a course suggested by a third party is to be preferred. It is for such reasons that conciliation has been the means by which more stable settlements have been reached than by any other course.

# 4

---

*The Nature and Handling of International Disputes*

---

The present international community clearly lacks instruments of government comparable to those which have become a generally accepted part of the institutional framework of most of the more highly developed states. It is possible, nevertheless, that the past half century has witnessed what in historical perspective will appear as a most rapid development in the institutions of international organization. First through bilateral and multilateral treaties, then through the League of Nations, and more recently through the United Nations, states have undertaken to adjust their political relations to the spectacularly rapid growth in the world's interdependence.

Many of these same treaties and conventions have contained special provisions for the settlement of disputes which might arise under them, or which otherwise might disturb the relations of the participating states. Through the League of Nations and now through the United Nations a substantial body of experience has been accumulated in the settlement of international disputes. In this chapter we will describe the manner in which disputes are now handled in the United Nations and indicate something of the importance of this recent experience. But first, let us look at the general nature of present-day international disputes.

## The Nature of International Disputes

A distinction is frequently made between those international disputes which appear to be suitable for judicial settlement and those which are more likely to be settled (or to have their settlement attempted) through some form of political negotiation.

No hard and fast line can be drawn between the two general groupings of disputes. However, those which have been submitted to arbitration or to judicial settlement have usually involved the interpretation of a treaty, of obligations of states under international law, or claims for reparations or for compensation. In many of these cases the disputants are concerned to get an interpretation of a legal right under a treaty to which they are a party.

Such disputes can be distinguished from those politico-economic disputes which bear more significantly on vital interests. Governments in their international affairs, like labor and management in national affairs, usually reserve as much freedom of action as possible in those matters which relate directly to their vital interests. If conflicts arise over such questions, nation-states in the international community and organizations in the national community usually wish to retain control not only over the terms of any settlement but also over the method through which settlement is attempted. In most cases they are unwilling to permit any kind of settlement by arbitration or judicial process. It is thus clear why mediation, which is based on the principle of voluntary agreement, has such an important role to play in the settlement of international disputes.

Despite the rapid growth in international organization during recent years, the nation-state is still the principal repository of political power. At the same time that nations seek dependable evidence that they can maintain and extend their security through world organization they continue to endeavor through unilateral or regional arrangements to create situations favorable to their security and to the patterns of economic and social life which they seek to promote. It is to be expected, therefore, that a large number of international disputes will continue to arise out of the continuing competition of nation-states for what they believe to be their political and military security.

Many disputes arise out of the vast and complex network of international commercial life. Some of those conflicts are covered by arbitration agreements written into treaties. Others arise in circumstances in which no special commercial settlement machinery exists. Such disputes are usually caught up into the political processes and become matters of political negotiation.

The more difficult commercial and political disputes in the international community usually reflect the shifting expanse of international economic activity. In one century the focus of this activity may be in the Mediterranean, in another century it may be in Western Europe, in another it may be in North America and the great land mass of Asia. The development of new spheres of economic activity and the absorption or transformation of the old are indications of man's enterprise. The shifting tides of economic power which are the result, however, provide the setting in which the competition of nation-states for security is carried on. The great majority of so-called political disputes have their economic components related intimately to the shifting economic circumstances of the time. It is for this reason that we have used the term "politico-economic disputes."

The main body of this section on international disputes will be devoted to a discussion of the general arrangements under which certain of these more difficult conflicts are brought into mediation and to the procedures and techniques which are then employed in an effort to gain a settlement. Our discussion will of necessity be in general terms. Each dispute has its own peculiarities, based on the widely differing economic, political, and personal factors involved. We will be looking, however, for those elements which this international mediation experience has in common.

## The Types of Machinery through which Settlement Is Attempted

Under the Covenant of the League of Nations, great emphasis was placed on preventing war. The League Covenant provided that disputing states should observe certain procedures of pacific settlement, and especially the lapse of a specified period of time, before resorting to war in defense of their national interests. While Article 10 of the Covenant, under which Members of the League undertook "to respect and preserve against external aggression the territorial integrity and political independence of Members," was considered by many to be an important part of the League structure, the emphasis of the League in practice was on Article 11. This provided that "any war or threat of war, whether immediately affecting any of the Members of the League or not, is hereby declared a matter of concern to the whole League, and the League shall take any action that may be deemed wise and effectual to safeguard the peace of nations." It was under the broad grant of power in this article that the League Council undertook most of its dispute settlement work.

With the United Nations the peaceful settlement of disputes became more firmly established as a part of international organization. It not only became a principal purpose of the organization itself but member states in adhering to the Charter undertook to settle their disputes without resort to force. The commitments assumed by Members are explicit. Chapter I, Article 2, paragraph 3 reads: "All members shall settle their international disputes by peaceful means in such a manner that international peace and security, and justice, are not endangered." Paragraph 4 of the same article carries even farther the commitment to refrain from the use of force: "All Members shall refrain in their international relations from the threat or use of force against the territorial integrity or political independence of any State, or in any other manner inconsistent with the Purposes of the United Nations."

The Charter places the initial responsibility directly upon the parties to settle the dispute by means of their own choice, rather than suggesting an immediate recourse to the Security Council or the General Assembly. Chapter VI, Article 33, paragraph 1 states: "The parties to any dispute, the continuance of which is likely to endanger the maintenance of international peace and security, shall, first of all, seek a solution by negotiation, inquiry, mediation, conciliation, arbitration, judicial settlement, resort to regional agencies or arrangements, or other peaceful means of their own choice." Failure of the parties to make sufficient effort at direct settlement may give rise to objection to the consideration of the dispute by one of the political organs of the United Nations or to a referral of the dispute back to the parties for continued direct efforts.

It is frequently most difficult, however, for states, parties to a serious dispute, to settle the dispute through bilateral negotiation, or as a result of direct negotiation to agree to submit the dispute to mediation or to arbitration.

In certain cases the settlement of disputes is covered by bilateral treaties. The infrequency with which such instruments have been invoked is an indication of the difficulties inherent in this approach to peaceful settlement. Bilateral agreements between states to settle disputes by mediation have been noticeably unsuccessful. The mediation process is usually reserved for those disputes of major concern to states and it has customarily taken the framework and encouragement of international organization to get this type of dispute into mediation.

Some disputes have been settled through regional machinery such as the Organization of American States. While it is open to question whether in the long run a decentralized approach is likely to gain favor as the general pattern for peaceful settlement, it would appear that more substantial efforts might be made to make use of regional machinery for the handling of disputes whose repercussions lie primarily with the region. In view of the large numbers of problems that have been placed before the United Nations it would take a very marked development in this direction for regional machinery to detract from the vigor of the more comprehensive world organization. The world has become so interdependent that any serious dispute in one particular region of the world is likely to be a matter of general international concern and one therefore which is considered appropriate for handling by the more universal organization.

**General responsibility of the United Nations Security Council and General Assembly.** The United Nations Charter provides differing methods for the settlement of international disputes, depending upon the nature of the dispute. In the case of so-called legal disputes, the Charter provides for recourse to the International Court of Justice. In Article 36 of the Statute of the International Court legal disputes concerning interpretation of a treaty are recognized as disputes particularly appropriate for the settlement procedures of the International Court. Such disputes may be distinguished from those which, according to the Charter, are appropriate for settlement through the Security Council and the

General Assembly. Under Chapter VI these organs handle disputes the continuance of which is likely to endanger the maintenance of peace, *i.e.*, disputes likely to have repercussions beyond the confines of the immediate relations of the parties concerned. If, therefore, the central political organs provide a service of settlement, it is a service provided less in the interests of the parties involved than in the interests of the international community.

It was the purpose of the United Nations Charter to ensure that the Security Council and the General Assembly should not be encumbered with the settlement of disputes which states might reasonably be expected to settle between themselves, nor be burdened with those disputes which, because they turn around questions of law or of fact, might appropriately be submitted to arbitration or to the International Court. The general approach which was intended was not unlike that which, in labor disputes, separates the handling of disputes under a contract and disputes over a new contract or over questions not covered by a contract. In practice, however, the United Nations has been most hesitant about refusing to proceed with the consideration of any international questions submitted to it, but rather has proceeded on the basis that the very submission of a dispute by a member state provides grounds for deeming it a matter with which the central political organ in question should concern itself.

The Security Council has primary responsibility for the preservation of peace. The Council under Chapter VII has the power to invoke economic and even military measures. The General Assembly, on the other hand, can only make recommendations, but these recommendations, when backed by the power of a sizable part of world public opinion, may be very effective.

With the outbreak of armed conflict in Korea and the series of measures taken by the United Nations in an effort to deal with it, the stage was set for a much more active role on the part of the General Assembly. In the initial stages the armed conflict in Korea was handled by the Security Council. The General Assembly had, however, been dealing with the problem of the independence of Korea for four years. When the conflict broke out a Commission previously established by the General Assembly was already on the spot. The report of that body to the Fifth Session of the Assembly provided a means for the Assembly to consider the broad aspects of the problem, the military aspects of which were before the Security Council. With the Soviet veto in the Security Council on November 30, 1950, of a resolution consequent to the intervention in Korea by the People's Republic of China, and the subsequent inclusion on December 6, 1950, of the same item on the agenda of the General Assembly, a first step was taken in discharging the responsibilities envisaged in the Uniting for Peace resolution adopted by the General Assembly on November 3, 1950. Under this resolution if the Security Council, because of lack of unanimity of the permanent members, fails to exercise its primary responsibility for the maintenance of international peace and security in any case where there appears to be a threat to the peace, breach of the peace, or act of aggression, the General Assembly shall consider the matter immediately with the view to making appropriate recommendations to Members for collective measures, including in the case of a breach of the peace or act of aggression, the use of armed force when necessary, to maintain or restore international peace and security. If not in emergency special session at the time, the General Assembly may meet in emergency special session within twenty-four hours of the request therefor.

Such an emergency special session is to be called if requested by the Security Council on a vote of any seven Members, or by a majority of the Members of the United Nations. Before the passage of this resolution it had been felt that military force could be used only on Security Council order or by great power agreement under Article 106.[1]

It is probable that under the Uniting for Peace resolution an increase will take place in the work of the General Assembly. As was the case in the secondary stages of the Korean conflict, serious controversies may now be dealt with in a forum where no great power has a veto and where a two-thirds majority can make recommendations. It is likely, however, that much of the previous experience of the Security Council will be relevant to the work of the General Assembly under its new powers. The Council has undertaken its work in the peaceful settlement of disputes primarily under Chapter VI. Under this chapter the powers of the Security Council are limited to making recommendations for settlement. In its work in the settlement of disputes the Assembly is engaged in much the same type of activity. In both cases there is a heavy dependence upon persuasion and recommendation as the principal means of bringing the conflict to an end and gaining a settlement.

### General Practices and Techniques of the Security Council and the General Assembly

**Submission and initial handling of disputes.**  A dispute may be submitted to the United Nations not only by one of the parties, but also by any Member. This had been the practice since the signature of the Covenant of the League, and is a token of the concern of the international community in any dispute which arises. The dispute is submitted by means of a communication to

[1] Article 106 provides for consultation and possible joint action on the part of the five major powers, on behalf of the United Nations, pending the coming into force of agreements for making armed forces available to the Security Council.

the Secretary-General which requests him to place the dispute before the Security Council or the General Assembly. There is no set form for this communication. Agenda items for the General Assembly must now be accompanied by at least an explanatory memorandum.

The submission of the dispute to the Security Council or the General Assembly does not mean that further efforts at direct settlement by the parties are precluded. It usually means only that direct negotiations have failed to bring a settlement and that a deadlock has been reached. Direct negotiations are commonly urged at every stage of the dispute whether it is under consideration by one of the principal political organs or by a special commission, subsequently established.

One of the more important questions concerns the timing of United Nations intervention. After positions become rigid, particularly when they are publicly taken, the task of settlement is rendered much more difficult. The propaganda mill has usually been working at top speed in justification of the positions so taken. An emphasis on the exhaustion of efforts at direct settlement before United Nations procedures are invoked is an operative premise of present international political organization, but it has a tendency to develop in the parties final positions and rigid views that render retreat and compromise more difficult. The general development of international organization has been such that a dispute normally does not come up for consideration unless it has undergone the preliminary processes of exchange of diplomatic notes and direct or regional attempts at settlement. In other words, it undergoes a process of crystallization and rigidity before it comes up for treatment at the international level. There is in international organization no regularized notice, as in labor disputes, of a failure to reach agreement and of the existence of a situation of potential concern to the public welfare.

The majority of international disputes undergo a process of crystallization and achieve a rigidity before they are submitted to the United Nations.

When submitted by a member state, the dispute is first placed on the provisional agenda of the Security Council or the General Assembly. As the Council or the Assembly moves toward adoption of the provisional agenda and a decision as to whether it will take some action in respect to the dispute, one or more Members directly concerned may claim that the dispute is a domestic one and thus outside the scope of the political organ. Such claims were made, for example, by the Netherlands in the initial stages of the Indonesian conflict, by India in the case of Hyderabad, and by South Africa on the question of the treatment of Indians in South Africa.

If the competence of the political organ is challenged the problem may be referred to the International Court. It is the usual practice, however, to proceed on the basis of a consensus or on the understanding that the problem of competence may be debated subsequently. It is seldom that the Security Council or the General Assembly has returned later to debate such a question. The fact that a dispute is of a sufficiently serious character to be drawn to the attention of the United Nations by a member state has usually weighed heavily in the decision to accept the provisional agenda and to proceed with consideration. By its subsequent action and resolutions the political organ then demonstrates its attitude toward its competence even though specific reference in a resolution is seldom made.

**The role and limitations of general debate.** The usual initial procedure of the Security Council or the General Assembly has been to engage in a general debate on the dispute. This is designed to provide an understanding of the issues involved and to clarify the positions taken by the disputants. A serious effort on the part of the Council or the Assembly to understand the nature of the dispute is a prerequisite to the development of methods for dealing with it. It is a requirement of the Charter that parties to the dispute shall be invited to participate in the discussion in the Security Council. Similar arrangements are made occasionally for especially concerned nonmembers and nongovernmental bodies. Other Members of the United Nations whose interests are affected are also invited to participate. Generally, the complainant state or states are first asked to make their statements and these are followed by statements of the other parties. At the close of these opening remarks, representatives of the Security Council or of the General Assembly can make statements and ask questions of the parties.

In some cases special steps are taken to elucidate the issues involved by setting up small subcommittees to collect evidence. Such steps were taken in connection with the Spanish question, the question of incidents in the Corfu Channel, and more informally in connection with the Berlin question.

The value of this initial procedure to the ultimate settlement of the dispute has been differently assessed. The initial debate is of importance in that it provides the means whereby the main points of the dispute can be brought out in the open and the international community can then bring influences to bear on the parties. The parties are made aware at an early date of the degree of political opposition or support which they are likely to encounter and the assumption is that a party may modify its position when it finds that its cause is received with marked disfavor. Thus the exercise of pressure on the parties is implicit in the initial debate. The debate, on the other hand, may have the disadvantage of causing the parties prematurely to define their positions and so may hinder rather than promote conciliation.

The present system for the pacific settlement of disputes is based upon the assumption of the paramount interest of the international community in the settlement of any dispute. The consideration of it by the Security Council or the General Assembly is at present the symbol of the concern of that community. The two political organs are forums which are utilized by parties directly and indirectly concerned to express their views on the issues of the dispute. They thereby become instruments for the organization and operation of public opinion. In many cases this has been undoubtedly a most potent weapon. As we shall note in the following sections, however, it has not always been easy to combine this role with that of the more direct mediation efforts.

**Use of the Chairman or President, or of a rapporteur.** There has been a growing tendency for private negotiations under the auspices of the Security Council to precede the general debate. In dealing with the India-Pakistan question in 1948 it was agreed, immediately after the initial statements by the parties, that private conversations should be held between the two parties under the auspices of the President. These private conversations continued over a considerable period of time. Certain agreements were reached, and the recommendations resulting from these conversations were reported to the Security Council and formed the basis of action taken by the Council. At a later stage during the consideration of the report of the Council's Commission, the Council resorted to this same procedure. General MacNaughton (President of the Council and the representative of Canada) carried on extensive discussions with the parties in an effort to secure agreement on the method for settling the dispute. A similar practice was followed in the General Assembly in connection with the Greek question in 1948 and 1949.

On May 24, 1950, the Security Council passed a resolution in which it undertook in its future activities to give consideration to a suggestion, which had come from a study of League of Nations experience, that the parties to a dispute be invited to meet with a representative of the Security Council, acting as a rapporteur or conciliator for the case "not later than immediately after the opening statements" in the Security Council on behalf of the parties concerned. Although the timing of this new procedure was as indicated, it was apparently the intention of several delegations that such action should normally be taken even before the opening public statements were made.

**The establishment of subsidiary machinery.** The Security Council or the General Assembly is seldom itself in a position to examine the details of the position of either party or, offhand, to suggest a solution. Its main task at this early stage is to get the parties to agree on certain principles and to accept the creation of special machinery for the elucidation of facts or of a mediatory body to aid in negotiating a substantive settlement. It is here that the mediatory functions of the Council or the Assembly are most clearly noticeable in the initial handling of the dispute, and the attitude of the parties is usually taken into the fullest account. In a certain sense the political organ attempts to negotiate with the parties the terms of a mediation agreement, especially adapted to the particular dispute.

The parties to the dispute usually believe that their vital interest is at stake in the procedure established in an effort to gain a settlement. They thus do not wish, in any arrangement for mediation, to be placed in the position where the essential features of their case would be endangered, or where they would be embarrassed before the public, by being held responsible for any subsequent breakdown of negotiations.

In most cases they are already sensitive at having their dispute brought before an international agency. The submission of a dispute to the United Nations in itself may be taken to imply an accusation that at least one of the parties is affecting adversely the maintenance of international peace. This implied accusation can cause resentment in the early stages of United Nations consideration, and frequently has done so.

If the dispute has already broken into open conflict, it is likely to be taken first to the Security Council. Measures are then attempted to prevent the spread of the conflict. The Council may order a truce, leaving the supervision of its resolution, the working out of a standstill agreement, the demarcation of truce lines, etc., to the specially created subsidiary body. In the background of such action by the Security Council lies the coercive power authorized under Chapter VII, but being a formal body, subject to pressure of time and aware of its unique world-wide position, the intervention of the Security Council is usually of a formal nature, guarded and wary. The intervention of either the Security Council or the General Assembly has at every stage to take account of national sovereignty and of the legal and practical limitations to United Nations action. The organ must keep in mind the fact that a formal and complete rejection of its proposals may damage its prestige.

In disputes in which it appears that some formal action of the Security Council or the General Assembly is required the Council or the Assembly may have to proceed along one or more of the following lines. Which of these types of action is used, its timing, and the order in which it is taken, varies according to the circumstances of the dispute.

These main types are:

1. Establishment or dispatch of a commission of investigation to ascertain the facts—usually on the spot.
2. Provisions for cessation of hostilities.
3. Measures with a view to settlement of the substance of the dispute.

**A commission of investigation.**   A commission of investigation is occasionally sent out to ascertain the actual facts of the dispute. In addition to its contact with governments, such a commission may receive local evidence through the hearing of witnesses. It may establish investigating teams or observation groups. This has given rise to special problems in connection with the treatment of communications, the selection of witnesses, the hearing of evidence, and the organization of investigation teams or observation groups.

It is the usual practice to request commissions of investigation to submit to the parent body recommendations based on the evidence which has been gathered, suggesting the next steps which should be taken by that body looking toward the solution of the dispute. Examples of United Nations commissions of investigation are the Commission of Investigation on Greek Frontier Incidents, which was set up by the Security Council in 1946, and the United Nations Special Committee on Palestine, created by the General Assembly in 1947.

The General Assembly in November, 1950, took a new step in this respect by creating a standing Peace Observation Commission. The Commission is composed of 14 Members of the United Nations. The Security Council may utilize the Commission, or if the Security Council is "not exercising the functions assigned to it by the Charter," the General Assembly or the Interim Committee may, upon a two-thirds vote, and with the consent of the state into whose territory it would go, send the Commission to "observe and report on the situation in any area where there exists international tension the continuance of which is likely to endanger the maintenance of international peace and security."

**Provisions for the cessation of hostilities.**   When fighting has already broken out, the Security Council or the General Assembly is faced with the task of achieving a cease-fire and restoring order. Under Chapter VII the Council is empowered to take coercive measures to secure compliance with its decisions in this respect. Until the Korean conflict broke out in June, 1950, the Security Council had relied far more upon negotiation and persuasion as a means of restoring peace, than upon any use of its power to institute international police measures.

The successive measures taken with a view to the restoration or the maintenance of peace tend to follow a general pattern.

Resolution calling upon the parties to refrain from action tending to aggravate the situation.

Resolution calling upon the parties to cease fire or to withdraw to certain lines.

Measures to bring about compliance with the cease-fire resolution.

Resolution empowering the organ charged with the settlement of the dispute to effect a truce. This fourth state involves the establishment of special machinery for arranging and supervising the truce, and may include the establishment of lines of demarcation between opposing forces, the appointment of military observers to report on violations of the truce, and the establishment of a special military body to assess the reports of local military observers.

**Measures for settlement.** The parent organ determines the general procedure which should be followed with a view to settlement. These initial decisions of procedure may be accompanied by a delimitation of the scope or basis of negotiations, with an indication of priorities and of measures to be taken by the individual parties. These may include:

*A return to direct negotiation:* This recommendation is commonly accompanied by the request that the central organ be kept informed of the course and outcome of the negotiations.

*Reference to the International Court:* This procedure has thus far been used in only one instance in connection with the dispute in incidents in the Corfu Channel. In this case the Security Council recommended that the parties should refer the question to the International Court.

*Establishment of subsidiary organs to assist in the settlement of disputes:* A subsidiary organ may be set up to assist the parties in the solution of their dispute. Many disputes have been handled in this manner. The General Assembly and the Security Council have established such organs in connection with the Indonesian, Palestine, India-Pakistan, Balkan, and Korean questions.

Since a large part of this chapter is devoted to the operations of these subsidiary organs, it may be useful to mention here the various organs which have been established by the United Nations to assist in the settlement of disputes:

*Indonesian Question:* A Committee of Good Offices was established in accordance with the Security Council resolution of August 25, 1947. This Committee continued to function through 1948. Following the outbreak of hostilities at the end of that year, the Committee was reconstituted as the United Nations Commission for Indonesia with additional terms of reference (January 28, 1949).

*India-Pakistan Question:* The United Nations Commission for India and Pakistan was established by the Security Council in the early part of 1948. On March 14, 1950, the Commission was replaced by the United Nations Representative for India and Pakistan. Sir Owen Dixon of Australia was appointed to the office on April 12, 1950. Upon the resignation of Sir Owen Dixon, a new resolution was adopted (March 31, 1951) and Dr. Frank Graham of the United States took over the duties of the United Nations Representative.

*Korean Question:* The first of the commissions established by the General Assembly to deal with this question was the United Nations Temporary Commission on Korea (November 14, 1947). This Commission was to observe and report on elections in Korea. At the next session of the Assembly the United Nations Commission on Korea was established (December 12, 1948). This organ continued to function until October 7, 1950, at which time the Assembly established the United Nations Commission for the Unification and Rehabilitation of Korea.

*Balkan Question:* The problems arising from the Greek frontier incidents were first dealt with by the Security Council. When proposals based upon the report of the Council's commission of investigation were vetoed in the Council, the problem was transferred to the General Assembly. The Assembly established the United Nations Special Committee on the Balkans on October 21, 1947. This Committee has been continued by the Assembly at each of its subsequent sessions.

*Palestine Question:* The first of the United Nations subsidiary organs to deal with the Palestine question was an investigating commission set up by the General Assembly (United Nations Special Committee on Palestine, May 15, 1947). The United Nations Palestine Commission was established at the next session of the Assembly as an integral part of the partition plan (November 29, 1947). When the question was next considered at a special session, this Commission was relieved of its functions and the office of United Nations Mediator was created (May 14, 1948). Count Folke Bernadotte of Sweden was appointed to the office. Following the assassination of the Mediator, Dr. Ralph Bunche became the Acting Mediator. While the Acting Mediator continued in office, primarily for the purpose of concluding the armistice agreements, the Assembly on December 11, 1948, established the United Nations Conciliation Commission for Palestine. Under this resolution and resolutions adopted by the Assembly in 1949 and 1950, this Commission has continued to seek a peaceful settlement of the Palestine question.

There have been numerous other subsidiary organs which either the Security Council or the General Assembly has established to assist it in the handling of the questions brought before the United Nations. These organs have carried out a wide variety of special functions in connection with the implementation of resolutions. [See in particular the UN Korean Reconstruction Agency (1950), the UN Relief for Palestine Refugees (1948), the Consular Commission in Batavia (1947), the UN Commissioners for Libya (1949) and for Eritrea (1950).] While many of these organs have made significant contributions to the handling of the political problems which the United Nations has faced, their tasks have not been primarily of a mediatory nature and their activities have, therefore, less relevance for the purposes of this comparative study.

**The selection of a mediator or a small commission.**   The general attributes of a good mediator would appear to be very much the same as in the labor field. However, as the Security Council or the General Assembly moves toward the appointment and composition of a commission, or the selection of a single mediator, there is a tendency for diplomatic bargaining.

The mediator may be a group, such as the Commission on India and Pakistan (Kashmir), the Commission on Korea, or the Committee of Good Offices (Indonesia), or it may be an individual like the Mediator for Palestine. Although the Committee of Good Offices was composed of three members, at many points its operations approximated those of a single mediator because two of the members were selected by the parties and in the early stages were especially sensitive to their interests, leaving the impartial third member, selected by the other two, with the necessity of exercising considerable initiative.

The mediatory commission may be made up of individuals "instructed" by their respective governments, or "uninstructed" individuals selected on the basis of purely personal qualifications. Count Bernadotte and Ralph Bunche in Palestine, and Sir Owen Dixon and Dr. Frank Graham in Kashmir, are examples of uninstructed mediators.

There seems to be a tendency to regard an individual or a very small group as better suited for undertaking conciliatory and mediatory functions at the secondary level. In many instances, an "uninstructed" individual may be the best instrument. The United Nations experience at this point would appear to closely parallel experience in labor disputes. The single mediator, appointed by the United Nations, can with ease visit the various centers in which mediation activities need to be undertaken, whereas a commission will tend to be accompanied by large staffs. The single mediator is also able to decide more rapidly the procedures which he will follow, whereas a commission will spend much more time in establishing and reviewing its procedures. It is of interest in this connection that in the case of the Commission on India and Pakistan, the Commission recommended its own dissolution and the appointment of a single mediator. It stated: "The Commission doubts whether a five-member body is the most flexible and desirable instrument to continue in the task." It suggested that "a single person can now more effectively conduct the negotiations, which, to be successful, must be carried out in active and constant consultation with the two parties. The designation of a single person with broad authority and undivided responsibility offers a more practical means of finding the balanced compromise necessary to advance the settlement of the dispute."[2]

The single mediator usually loses no time in assuming his responsibilities upon appointment. Procedural delays may occur in the case of a commission and allowance has to be made for some delay. The general feeling that the mediation processes should commence before the crystallization of a dispute is justified to some extent by United Nations experience in Kashmir. The delay in the commission getting under way was probably a handicap to its work.

In April, 1949, the United Nations General Assembly accepted a proposal which had come from its Interim Committee for the establishment of an International Panel for Inquiry and Conciliation. The proposal provided that each member state of the United Nations should nominate not more than five persons to constitute a Panel from which the Secretary-General, the President of the General Assembly, or the Chairman of the Interim Committee

[2]U.N. Document S/1430.

could select persons or commissions to perform tasks of inquiry or conciliation. It was provided that the members of the Panel "shall not, in the performance of their duties, seek or receive instructions from any Government."

The establishment of the Panel of Conciliators shows the development of the idea of "uninstructed" mediation. The Panel was first drawn upon by the Security Council when it appointed Dr. Frank Graham, one of the United States nominees to the Panel, as United Nations Representative for India and Pakistan.

### Practices and Techniques of Subordinate Bodies

The United Nations mediation activities must be viewed as a series of parallel and coordinated efforts taking place at different levels. The functions of the parent body and the subsidiary organs are closely intertwined and supplement each other. At no stage of the handling of the dispute does the parent body absolve itself of its major responsibility for the preservation or the maintenance of peace. The activities of its subsidiary body are usually followed closely. The parent body may step in from time to time, resulting in a back-and-forth handling of the dispute.

The field agency usually takes over the detailed negotiations. It operates in a totally different medium from the parent organ. It is not so formal and it has a greater internal flexibility. Moreover, its nearness to the area of dispute and to the disputants themselves, its daily contacts with their problems, make it an instrument most suitable for the handling of such delicate problems as truce preservation and the negotiation of settlements. The experience of the United Nations field agencies, even under trying circumstances, as in Palestine and Indonesia, indicates the effectiveness of this method of operation.

**Interpreting the terms of reference.**  In setting up a subsidiary body to assist the parties to a dispute in working out a settlement, the United Nations has not only had to determine the type of body that would be most effective for a particular dispute, but it has had to decide on the frame of reference within which the body was to operate.

These subsidiary bodies have generally been given broad terms of reference. The Palestine Conciliation Commission was established in December, 1948, by the General Assembly to "achieve a final settlement of all questions outstanding." The Commission on India and Pakistan was instructed to investigate the facts and to exercise its good offices and mediation with a view to the restoration of peace and order and the holding of a plebiscite to decide the future of the State of Jammu and Kashmir. Where the subsidiary body is utilized also for the purpose of bringing about and supervising the truce, the Security Council resolutions on the question of the truce have been, at times, more specific.

The parent body has, nevertheless, usually allowed the field agency latitude in the interpretation of its tasks. For example, at its 313th meeting on June 3, 1948, the Security Council decided that the Mediator for Palestine should have full authority to act within the terms of the resolution of May 29, 1938, and to interpret it in any way he deemed correct. Only if that interpretation were challenged would the matter be submitted to the Council for further consideration. Subsequent directives to the Mediator and the Acting Mediator were based on this decision.

**Relations of commission members to home governments.** In cases in which governments are appointed to United Nations commissions, those persons serving on their behalf keep in close touch with the governments which they represent. The lead which each of them takes in the negotiations is not likely to be out of step with the home government and is frequently developed in the closest consultation with it. It is obvious that a mediation or conciliation arrangement of this kind imposes a heavy burden on the persons who serve on commissions. There is not only the difficulty of the commission being able to move expeditiously in a complicated political situation. There are the further problems resulting from the necessity for each representative to reconcile the national interest of his home government with the merits of the case in dispute as seen from the vantage point of direct field negotiation.

**Location of the commission.** An unusual flexibility has characterized the choice of a seat of operation by the commission. The United Nations Commission on India and Pakistan carried out its task in New Delhi and Karachi, separately and jointly, and then transferred its activities to Europe. The Mediator and Acting Mediator for Palestine based themselves in Rhodes, but kept up a concurrent and direct contact with the capitals of the parties. The United Nations Committee of Good Offices (Indonesia) followed a schedule of meeting for about three weeks in Jakarta and then for a similar period in Batavia. This shifting of the seat of negotiations went on from the signing of the Renville agreement until the second "police action." The United Nations Commission for Indonesia in the later stages of its work participated in the Hague Conference, but maintained alternate delegates in Indonesia. The first United Nations Representative for India and Pakistan, while operating from Srinigar, visited Karachi, New Delhi, and the scene of the disturbances in Jammu and Kashmir.

**Relations with the parties.** The subsidiary body must promptly establish a relationship with the disputants and with concerned Members of the United Nations. The resolution setting up the body generally urges upon all parties to provide all facilities to the commission or the mediator. In practice, many of the details are worked out within the region in which the subsidiary body is operating. Much is left to the initiative of the field unit and to the disputants themselves.

Area surveys in the region of the dispute for purposes of both truce and negotiation are usually the preliminary steps. These area surveys may or may not be carried out with the assistance of the disputants. When there is a tense situation travel facilities may present a great problem. In this respect Ralph Bunche (Palestine) and Sir Owen Dixon (Kashmir) have commended the cooperation they received from the parties.

In cases where one of the parties to the dispute has not accepted the decision of the parent body to set up a commission, or has challenged its terms of reference, the subsidiary body has later on been considerably hampered by lack of cooperation or even directly hindered. At times this has led to a partial suspension of its activities (United Nations Temporary Commission on Korea, United Nations Special Committee on Palestine, United Nations Special Committee on the Balkans). In the case of the United Nations Representative for India and Pakistan, however, the conditional acceptance of the mediatory plan did not prevent considerable cooperation by the parties in the work in the field.

Where an actual boycott of the commission has been declared by one of the parties, the commission has always tried to keep itself open to an approach and has attempted to contact the dissentient by various means, *i.e.*, through the Secretary-General of the United Nations (UN Special Committee on the Balkans); asking the Secretary-General to forward a cablegram addressed to the government of the U.S.S.R. requesting the latter to lend its good offices to help establish contact between the commission and leading personalities in North Korea (UN Temporary Commission on Korea); dispatch of a letter, on two occasions, to a general in North Korea (UN Temporary Commission on Korea).

Where the commission has had to operate amidst actual conflict, it has been faced with the problem of maintaining direct and regular contact with the parties so as to ascertain their views on a rapidly changing situation. This is allied to the general problem of transmission of views and proposals between the parties, and between the parties and the commission. The request to appoint liaison officers may come from the parent organ, from the commission (UN Special Committee on the Balkans) or from the parties. The commission's functions as an intermediary have been performed in various ways, *i.e.*, an individual representative from the committee at the time of breakdown of negotiations acted as intermediary for an exchange of letters between the parties (Committee of Good Offices, Indonesia); the United Nations staff of the Mediator acted as intermediary for transmission of communications between the Mediator and the parties concerned (Mediator and Acting Mediator for Palestine). For a discussion of the views submitted by one party to it, the commission may proceed as a body to the headquarters of the other party (UN Commission on India and Pakistan) or it may send individual members. This frequent movement has been characteristic of the activities of the single mediator (Palestine, India and Pakistan). A practice to be noted is that of the UN Commission on India and Pakistan delegating one of its members to place himself at the disposal of the two governments for the purpose of clarifying the Commission's proposals. Where it has been possible to get an agreement on a joint meeting, such a meeting has been promptly convened. In one instance, however, because of failure to get agreement on the agenda, the Commission unfortunately abandoned the joint conference.

**Responsibility for initiating suggestions.** There has been considerable variation in the roles which commissions have played in their attempt to achieve a long-term settlement. It has seemed most desirable for the commission to play an active part, not only in bringing the parties together and transmitting proposals, but in attempting to find a *via media* between conflicting proposals and in putting forth its own suggestions and proposals.

In the negotiations much depends upon the attitudes of the parties, their relations with the commission, and the commission's general approach. It is crucial for the commission, or the single mediator, to understand when to step in, and when to step out and let the two parties settle their dispute or various aspects of it directly. It has been maintained in this respect that the work of the Palestine Conciliation Commission might have proceeded more rapidly if it had followed a more flexible plan of operation.

As in labor disputes, it would seem that the first general task of a subsidiary body was to find the initial areas of agreement between the parties and to base itself firmly upon these agreements even though they may be of a minor character. As the negotiations proceed the subsidiary body attempts to enlarge these areas of agreement, while narrowing down the areas of disagreement. Usually, some area of agreement is apparent from the initial discussions that follow the submission of the dispute to the Security Council. Thus, in the Kashmir question, it was evident that the parties were in general agreement that a plebiscite should be held to determine the future of Jammu and Kashmir, and also that they were both concerned to settle the dispute by pacific methods. In the Indonesian question, both parties were agreed upon the goal of setting up a future state in Indonesia with some form of federal relationship with the mother country.

In the initial efforts to establish an area of agreement, the subsidiary bodies have exhibited considerable initiative and resourcefulness. It is at the stage where the area of agreement must be expanded, so as to embrace the major points at dispute, that the tasks of the subsidiary body become highly delicate and complicated.

Perhaps the major problem in this sphere has been how to determine the degree of responsibility which the commission (or mediator) should take for the initiation of suggestions calculated to lead to a settlement of the dispute. This also has its parallel in labor disputes. The pattern of action in the United Nations has ranged from very modest assumptions of the commission's role in the negotiations to a high degree of initiative in the form of suggestions and proposals. Much depends upon the commission's interpretation of its own terms of reference in this respect. The Mediator for Palestine, in interpreting his role, felt that he should be the first authority to whom all complaints regarding the truce arrangement should be directed and, in this interpretation, he was upheld by the Security Council.

The Committee of Good Offices (Indonesia) was hampered at the outset by the limited definition which it gave to its functions: namely, that it would make suggestions only if requested to do so by the parties. One party requested the Committee to take an active part, and even to suggest a basis of settlement, but the other party was prepared at first to receive suggestions from the Committee only on questions of procedure. The Committee at first held separate meetings with each of the parties in the hope of persuading them to present constructive proposals of their own. When it was found that this procedure did not elicit proposals looking toward a settlement, the Committee found it necessary to break the stalemate by putting forward its own comprehensive proposal. The Committee thereafter received informal replies to its suggestions and discussed them separately with the parties at informal meetings. Only at a later stage was it distinctly understood that the Committee had the power to make, and even to publish, its suggestions to the parties without waiting for them to invite the Committee to do so.

The United Nations Commission for Indonesia, which succeeded the Committee of Good Offices, played a more active role, partly because of previous experience and partly on account of its own approach, based on new terms of reference which specifically authorized it to make suggestions. It convened the initial joint meetings in Batavia under its direct auspices, and informally suggested points for consideration in connection with the restoration of the Republic government to Jogjakarta. However, occasionally, private and informal conversations between the parties were resorted to, the Commission being kept informed of the progress of the discussions. At the Hague Round Table Conference the Commission arranged for its participation in the Conference to be clearly defined in the Rules of Procedure. The general position of the Commission at the Conference was set forth in Article 3, which provided that "the United Nations Commission for Indonesia will participate in the Round Table Conference in accordance with its terms of reference, as they have been established by the Security Council." The Commission was authorized to participate in all meetings of the Steering Committee and it was mandatory that the provisional agenda should include "every subject in respect of which the head of one of the delegations or the United Nations Commission has submitted a request for a discussion." These two provisions permitted the Commission to take the initiative at any time in the activities of the Conference.

At all stages of the work of the Conference, the Commission took an active part by attending formal meetings and by participating in the informal talks. For the most part, the Commission preferred not to intervene before the parties had been given full opportunity to reach agreement among themselves. When such agreement was not forthcoming, the Commission then exercised its functions of mediation.

Especially during the concluding stages of the Conference, the parties turned to the Commission for advice. The Commission then made substantial suggestions designed both to expedite the procedure of the Conference and to promote the settlement of major issues. The Commission's assistance was instrumental in reaching agreement on all principal points.

The approach of Sir Owen Dixon, the United Nations Representative for India and Pakistan, was very definite as to his role in the negotiations. This was partly due to the mandate given him by the Security Council and to the specific nature of his task, which was to bring about an agreement on the demilitarization proposals as a precondition to the holding of a plebiscite. In this task he was asked to bear in mind the proposals of General Mac-Naughton of Canada, who, as President of the Security Council, had conducted private talks with the two parties.

Sir Owen Dixon reports: "I had formed an opinion that my best course was to deal with the Prime Ministers and if possible bring them together at a meeting with me at which a sustained effort might be made to effect a settlement." A joint meeting was agreed upon and lasted for five days. "At the opening of the meeting I informed the two Prime Ministers that as far as I was concerned they could talk with the utmost freedom, because, subject to one qualification, what they said need not be disclosed. That qualification was that, if my Mission failed, I must report to the Security Council the nature of the proposals made and rejected, and if, on the other hand, agreement was reached, the agreement would of course be reported. . . . I found that neither country had any affirmative plans or proposals which her Prime Minister wished to put forward. I therefore proceeded to describe the course which I would propose to them."[3] In this and in subsequent meetings with the parties various plans for demilitarization and partial plebiscite were suggested by Sir Owen but agreement was not secured.

Substantial initiative in negotiations was also taken by Count

[3]Report of Sir Owen Dixon to the Security Council, U.N. Document S/1791, September 15, 1950

Bernadotte, United Nations Mediator in Palestine, and by Ralph Bunche, who succeeded him as Acting Mediator. An interesting expedient was adopted by Count Bernadotte and Dr. Bunche. Their discussions for political settlement commenced with discussions with each of the parties in Cairo, Amman, Damascus, Beirut, and Tel Aviv. They thereafter resorted to the expedient of inviting the two parties to make available to them experts, not for political discussions but for technical information concerning their respective positions. These consultations between the Mediator and the experts made it possible for him to put forward his suggestions, to elicit replies thereon from the parties, and thereafter to elicit comments from the parties on the replies.

It seems agreed that one of the reasons for the success of Dr. Bunche's efforts was his willingness to put before the parties a stream of proposals. Through the replies to these proposals the respective positions of the parties were gradually clarified and the areas in which agreement was possible were slowly revealed. Throughout his negotiation the Acting Mediator insisted on his willingness to continue the discussions and to consider any proposals which might hold promise of peaceful settlement. A contrast is provided by another commission which, on finding that a plan formulated by it was rejected by one of the parties, left the scene of its activities after having stayed for only three months.

Some mention should be made of practices which have occasionally created a distrust in the minds of the parties toward the mediatory agency and thus lessened the confidence with which its initiative has been received. In one dispute, a member of the commission was designated to engage in discussion with the individual parties separately. Each party confronted him with different questions to which he replied by explanations regarding the interpretation placed by the commission on one of its proposals. Later the record of the conversations made it apparent that it was difficult to reconcile the explanations given to the parties in response to their questions. The confusion and uncertainty thereby created was a factor that contributed towards a stalemate in the activities of the mediating agency. Such cases only serve to emphasize the need for great care in the selection and in the conduct of all persons attached to the mediatory body.

**Formal and informal meetings.**  The question of informal and formal meetings arises not only with regard to the internal work of a commission but also in its relations with the parties. Where the mediating agency is a single person, the maximum of flexibility can be maintained. This same flexibility is difficult to maintain in the case of a commission. Informal meetings (of which no minutes are kept) if used with too great frequency, have time and again given rise to misunderstanding. The general practice appears to be that while informal meetings may be of assistance in reaching an agreed decision, the agreed decision should eventually be taken and registered in a formal meeting.

**Coordination of action with the parent body.**  At the outset a subsidiary body is faced with the question of keeping in touch with the political organ which established it. This is especially necessary in cases where it is also entrusted with the enforcement of the truce resolutions. In general, the parent organ is disinclined to become involved in the day-to-day developments of a dispute except when there is a crisis, and then only on the basis of a report from the mediator or commission. In this respect the relationship is very similar to that between a mediator or a commission appointed by the Federal Mediation and Conciliation Service in the United States and the regional or national office of the Service, or a nonstatutory Presidential fact-finding board and the office of the President. In the case of United Nations commissions of inquiry the relations between the parent organ and the commission are generally confined to setting up the commission and receiving the report. The political organ has usually endorsed the achievements of its field agencies and adopted their recommendations for further action.

The public relations of the field unit have always been a delicate subject. While it is desirable that United Nations activities be given publicity, the tendency of the field unit is to act confidentially until a definite position can be arrived at. Delicacy of the negotiations would seem to require such a guarded attitude. While all field units have to report to the parent organ, the nature of these reports during the time the unit is actually in operation is usually a matter within the discretion of the commission itself.

A distinction can be drawn between two types of reports which are presented to the principal organ during the course of negotiations: (1) reports which are submitted as a means of keeping the principal organ informed of general developments without attempting to go into detail, and (2) reports which are submitted with the intention of enlisting the authoritative support of the principal organ for certain activities of the commission. The latter are especially relevant to disputes where the supervision of a truce is proceeding simultaneously with long-term political negotiations. The timing of such reports, in the absence of explicit instructions from the principal organ, is a matter entirely at the discretion of the subsidiary body.

In its day-to-day work the field agency has relied largely on its own initiative and the cooperation of the parties to the dispute. It has, at times, however, called upon the parent body to assist in creating an atmosphere conducive to negotiation, especially where a breakdown in negotiations is threatened or where the intransigence of one party had delayed effective negotiation. This overall supervision or, more accurately, assistance, by the parent body has played an important role in the final settlement of the dispute. Assistance has been obtained not only by means of progress reports by the subsidiary body requesting action on the part of the Security Council, but also by means of personal appearances by representatives of the subsidiary body at Security Council meetings to explain or analyze these reports and suggestions.

In the Palestine conflict there was frequent and effective resort to these two practices. The Mediator and the Acting Mediator for Palestine frequently participated in the meetings of the Security Council and took an active part in formulating proposals for narrowing the area of dissent and expanding the area of agreement between the two parties. Acting on the reports and suggestions made by the Mediator or Acting Mediator, the Council on several occasions issued specific instructions with respect to truce supervision and in support of the mediation effort.

In the Indonesian question, after the "police action" of December, 1948, the Security Council, following the suggestions of the Committee of Good Offices, adopted a resolution insisting upon the unconditional release of the Republican leaders as a precondition to any further negotiations. In subsequent discussions in the Council, substantial pressure was put upon the Netherlands government for the release of the Republican leaders and the restoration of the Republican government.

This back-and-forth handling of a dispute is well illustrated in the handling of the Kashmir dispute. It was originally brought to the attention of the Security Council by the government of India on January 1, 1948. Between January 1 and June 3, 1948, the Kashmir question was debated and discussed in 33 meetings of the Security Council. In addition, private conferences were held by the successive Presidents of the Council with the representatives of India and Pakistan.

Following these discussions the negotiations were transferred to the Commission on India and Pakistan, which was instructed to exercise its good offices and mediation with a view to the restoration of peace and order and the holding of a plebiscite to decide whether the State of Jammu and Kashmir was to accede to India or Pakistan. The Commission was also instructed to keep the Security Council informed of its activities and of the development of the situation, to report to the Council concerning the implementation of the Council's resolutions, to submit conclusions and proposals, and to report to the Council whether the plebiscite, to be conducted by a United Nations nominee, had been free and impartial.

The Commission had numerous conversations with the representatives of India and Pakistan, and with representatives of other concerned governments, first on the subcontinent and then in Paris during the Third General Assembly, in an attempt to arrive at an agreement on principles for a plebiscite in Jammu and Kashmir. The proposals of the Commission were finally submitted to the representatives of India and Pakistan with the hope they would be accepted in their entirety. One of the members of the Commission was sent to India and Pakistan in order to provide the two governments with the necessary explanations. The proposals, with certain clarifications, were accepted and on January 1, 1949, the cease-fire went into effect. Shortly thereafter, the Commission returned to the subcontinent.

By July, 1949, the Commission was able to get an agreement on the demarcation of the cease-fire line, but by December, 1949, the Commission in a report to the Security Council suggested that the "possibilities of mediation open to it have been exhausted." The report focused attention on the specific problem of demilitarization and recommended that the Security Council appoint a single person for this task.

When this report came up for consideration, the Members of the Security Council thought that the best step would be for the President of the Security Council to meet informally with the two parties and examine with them the possibility of finding a mutually satisfactory basis for dealing with the Kashmir problem. It was pointed out "that does not derogate in any way from the powers of the Security Council. It does not remove the matter in any way from the powers of the Security Council. It does not remove the matter in any way from its purview; it merely prepares the work for it in the most efficient manner possible." The President of the Security Council had numerous conversations with the two parties between December 17 and December 29, 1949, at which later date he reported to the Council. As reported by him his main effort was not directed toward putting forward wholly new proposals, but in taking that part of the existing plan in connection with which difficulties had arisen and finding ways and means of resolving those problems. The President's efforts were an attempt to get further agreement on the principles laid down by the Commission and accepted by the parties.

When the President found that specific agreement on demilitarization as a precondition to holding the plebiscite was not within sight, the dispute was again taken up by the Security Council. Sir Owen Dixon was appointed as United Nations Representative and the handling of the dispute was then again transferred to the subcontinent. We have already noted his failure to get agreement. In March, 1951, the Security Council made a further effort to provide machinery for a settlement by passing a resolution again establishing the office of United Nations Representative. In April, 1951, Dr. Frank Graham was appointed to this post.

**Supporting action by member states.** In many of the United Nations mediation efforts previous to the outbreak of hostilities in Korea, the mediatory effort has been supported or supplemented through direct representations to the disputants by Members of the United Nations. These representations have been both informal and formal. They have ranged all the way from a private expression of views to, in one instance during the conflict in Palestine, a *démarche* by a major power that a further extension of hostilities in one area would be met by military force. In many instances these representations are not made public. In cases in which a United Nations commission is composed of governments it is the expectation that these governments will exercise a general diplomatic initiative in connection with the work of their representative on the commission.

In those instances in which single mediators have been appointed, the particular individuals have usually been selected because it was believed they could be relied upon to approach the dispute on its merits and without reference to any particular strategic interest which their country of origin might have. It does not follow, however, that individual United Nations mediators have not called for and received the support of direct and substantial diplomatic pressures from countries who have both a general and a strategic interest in a peaceful solution. This was especially the case in the Palestine conflict where national diplomatic pressures were brought to bear in efforts to restrain the parties and in attempts to neutralize other diplomatic forces which sought one form or another of partisan settlement. With the outbreak of hostilities in Korea and the direct involvement of military contingents from 15 member countries, the full range of the formal and informal governmental diplomatic galaxy was brought into play.

**Conclusion and supervision of a settlement.**   When a breach of the peace has occurred there are two main elements to a settlement. First, there are the necessary measures to stop hostilities. As we have noted, they may include cease-fire lines, armistices, and troop withdrawals. In bringing about the cessation of hostilities the mediator may have to use all the pressure at his disposal including reference to and support from the parent organ. However, the lasting political settlement which must follow the temporary military measures, in the nature of things, has to be built even more markedly upon the agreement of the parties. This agreement between the parties must be the constant objective of the mediator or conciliation commission.

If the basis for a settlement is found by the subsidiary body it is usually endorsed by the parent organ. Upon conclusion of a settlement the services of the commission may still be needed for some months. This may involve general policing of the settlement and perhaps United Nations observation or supervision of a plebiscite. An important feature of the activities of the United Nations Commission for Indonesia has been its general oversight over the fulfillment of the terms of the agreement arrived at at the Hague Conference. This follow-up action was made a part of the general agreement.

### Achieving a Cease-fire and Getting a Settlement

As we have indicated, in cases in which hostilities have broken out, the United Nations has the dual responsibility of achieving a cease-fire and of promoting successfully a settlement of the principal issues in dispute. In only two cases, in Korea and in Palestine, has the Security Council taken any steps under Chapter VII, and these were of a preliminary nature. That chapter permits the ordering of measures of forcible restraint. In the majority of cases the Council and the General Assembly have emphasized the mediatory character of their intervention. The Security Council has generally utilized the methods of Chapter VI even when it has had the difficult task of stopping hostilities as well as getting a settlement.

In most such cases these dual functions have been incorporated in the terms of reference of the subsidiary commissions (or the mediator). The operation of the subsidiary bodies in these fields has shown that the functions of bringing about a termination of hostilities and of assisting the parties to reach a substantive agreement are closely intertwined.

In the Palestine, Indonesian, and Kashmir questions, the Security Council was faced at some point in its considerations with the task of bringing about a termination of hostilities. In these three cases the subsidiary bodies set up to assist the parties to reach an agreement on the substance of the disputes, were utilized by the Security Council to bring about the compliance of the parties with the Council's cease-fire resolutions or otherwise to gain a cease-fire. The translation of Council resolutions into reality in the line of battle has required protracted and complicated negotiations by the subsidiary body which have involved the utmost tact and delicacy. Even where the parties have accepted the principle of the cease-fire, the military positions of the rival forces often make it highly inconvenient to either or both sides to maintain their positions over a period of time. To alleviate local tension it may be necessary to bring about detailed agreement between the parties on such questions as the demarcation of the cease-fire lines, the creation of demilitarized zones, the release of prisoners, the prevention of inflammatory propaganda, and machinery of supervision.

In the Palestine question, although the Mediator was informed by the President of the Security Council on June 2, 1948, that both parties had unconditionally accepted the terms of the first truce resolution by the Security Council, difficulties arose as to the specific interpretation of the truce resolution of May 29, 1948. Empowered by the Security Council to interpret the terms of the resolution, and after extensive discussions and negotiations with both parties carried on from June 3 to 6, 1948, the Mediator made certain interpretations of the resolution and certain decisions as to its application which were voluntarily accepted by both parties unconditionally on June 9, and the four-week truce went into effect on June 11, 1948.

In the Indonesian conflict the Committee of Good Offices immediately undertook preparations for the holding of political discussions, but at the same time arranged for the appointment by the parties of Special Committees to deal with questions of the cease-fire. These Committees were headed by civilian representatives assisted by high-ranking military representatives. The Committee of Good Offices put forward various suggestions for the implementation of the cease-fire, but the parties took sharply differing points of view and agreement was not possible. At a later stage when negotiations for a political settlement commenced, the problem of concluding a truce agreement was merged with that of establishing a basis for a political settlement.

The close interconnection between negotiations for implementing the cease-fire resolutions of the Security Council and negotiations for a long-term political settlement is also shown by the handling of these dual tasks by the United Nations Commission for Indonesia which succeeded the Good Offices Committee. Combined negotiations were carried on for some weeks in Batavia on the inteconnected issues of arrangements for the observance of the cease-fire, the restoration of the Republican government, and the holding of a Round Table Conference at The Hague. In these negotiations, the Commission played a vital role.

In the Kashmir question, although no cease-fire resolution was passed by the Security Council, the Commission was faced with the immediate task of bringing about a termination of hostilities. As a result of extensive negotiations with the parties, the Commission succeeded in getting cease-fire orders issued by the conflicting armies on January 1, 1949. This was made possible by persuading the parties to agree on general conditions for a truce and for an eventual plebiscite. In July, 1949, the Commission was able to obtain agreement between the military representatives of India and Pakistan, meeting in Karachi, on the demarcation of a cease-fire line. This line was a further step in the prevention of hostilities in Kashmir.

The close interrelation of the issues involved in achieving a cease-fire and getting a settlement are even more graphically illustrated by the United Nations experience in Korea. At its meeting on June 25, 1950, immediately following the invasion by North Korean forces, the Security Council called for the immediate cessation of hostilities and for the withdrawal of the North Korean forces to the 38th parallel. The United Nations Commission on Korea, which had been created by the General Assembly in 1948 and which since that time had been seeking a settlement between North and South Korea, was asked to observe the withdrawal and to report its fully considered recommendations with the least possible delay.

In the succeeding seven months a number of different proposals for the cessation of hostilities and for the settlement of the conflict were put forward in the United Nations in a highly charged political atmosphere. These efforts broke down, either over the separation which was projected between negotiations for a cease-fire and negotiations for a settlement, or over an inability to agree on the particular questions to be considered in the settlement discussions.

# 5

## *Some Areas of Comparability and Some Tentative Conclusions*

The successful resolution of a dispute through the process of mediation obviously depends upon far more than the quality of the mediator and the development and improvement of procedures and techniques of peaceful settlement. Conflicts in which the parties enter mediation with incompatible or mutually ex· clusive goals are clearly more difficult to settle than those in which significant common interests are readily apparent. It would also appear that disputes are very difficult to solve in which one or both of the conflicting parties believe that, because of the comparative power which lies at their command, there are no substantial risks in a failure to reach agreement.

Any public agency established to provide a service of mediation, whether governmental or intergovernmental must, however, give primary attention to the improvement of those tools over which it has control and which are available for its work. The range of disputes with which the agency in question has to deal may be wide, covering those of both major and minor character. It is for this reason that the preceding chapters have emphasized the governmental and intergovernmental procedures through which mediation is attempted. To avoid oversimplification these arrangements and procedures have been described in considerable detail. Some of the techniques have been suggested which mediators have found useful in facilitating an agreement. These have been developed especially in the parts which have dealt with the handling of labor conflicts.

We now come to the central question of the present study. Is the experience in the handling of labor and international disputes sufficiently comparable for any conclusions, even tentative, to be drawn as to the approaches, procedures, and techniques which in general have been found to facilitate a settlement?

### Similarities and Dissimilarities in the Two Settings

It is clear that in both fields of conflict the organized groups in dispute have been able to preserve for themselves considerable freedom of action within the governmental communities of which they are a part. This freedom of action has been preserved because the members of the group, whether of management or of labor, or of nation-states, have believed that they had a vital stake (and at times even a survival stake) in the terms of any settlement with other organized groups with whose interests they were in at least partial conflict.

There is no need to emphasize the limited degree to which the international community possesses political and legal institutions comparable to those which the national community can bring to bear to restrain parties in conflict. The basic institutional settings are not only widely separated on "the conflict scale," but the separation is increased as any country within the world community, in the face of what it believes to be an external or internal threat, either institutes emergency provisions for the settlement of labor disputes or finds effective ways to bring the force of an aroused public opinion to focus on those who are believed to threaten the public welfare. While there is in the international community a growing realization of the cost of conflict, there are as yet no comparable ways either of creating, in an international emergency, new and more forceful dispute-settling machinery, or of rapidly developing and focusing a world public opinion.

It has been suggested, nevertheless, that the larger labor and management units in the United States and in England, even in wartime, have been able to preserve considerable freedom of action. We have indicated some of the difficulties inherent in any attempt to facilitate a settlement by the employment of governmental force against such well-organized and established groups. We have noted the inconclusive result of government seizure in one recent railway dispute in the United States. Sir Frederick Leggett has referred to the miners who forced the government to abandon its attempt to enforce arbitration awards by fines and threats of prison sentences. Carl Christian Schmidt has spoken of the rejection of compulsory arbitration in Sweden as a useful means of settling labor conflicts. In all these countries it has been difficult, and in most cases impossible, to define the public interest in any terms which would remove from the more powerful management and labor units the primary responsibility for the settlement of their disputes.

It is obvious that the more substantial parallels exist between international disputes and those labor disputes of the type which create a public emergency. In these more difficult labor conflicts the goals of the contending parties are usually more incompatible, the power elements are more substantial, the positions have often become more rigid, and because of the larger and more complex units, retreat is often more difficult. This is not to say that mediation experience developed in the settlement of labor disputes of a lesser intensity may not have something to contribute to the techniques of international mediation. It would appear, however, that as labor conflicts move up the scale of power and intensity, and gain in their capacity to threaten the public welfare, more parallels develop with mediation experience in the international field. Our treatment of labor disputes in this study has been concerned principally with those not covered by arbitration contracts (approximately 10 per cent). Even in these the emphasis has been on those conflicts which have defied early settlement.

We have suggested in the Introduction and in the first part of Chapter 1 some of the additional reasons why it would not be surprising if the mediation experience in the two fields was found to have certain similarities. In each field the future status of the negotiators is frequently dependent upon the degree to which they can achieve the initially outlined goals. In many disputes in both areas the negotiators must carry sizable constituencies with them. In both fields organized groups in conflict must take account of public opinion and therefore are sensitive to their own relationship to the public as well as to the other party and the mediator. Conflicts in each field usually involve the balance of power between the disputants.

The negotiators in the two fields are dealing with issues which are usually very different in character. The issues in international disputes are often of long standing and have achieved a rigidity and an emotional intensity lacking in many if not most labor disputes. Labor conflicts usually involve disputes over wages,

Some comparative factors bearing on the mediation
of labor disputes.

Some comparative factors bearing on the mediation
of international disputes.

hours, and working conditions—matters of a very different qualitative order. As we have suggested, however, there is latent in these questions an emotional potential which, when compounded with the belief that fundamental rights or freedoms have been violated, has the possibility of creating a conflict of major proportions. In the free economies of the West these questions of a man's relationship to his job have not been closely prescribed by law. The freedom which has been retained for the voluntary agreement of well-organized economic groups is obviously a result both of the rigorous protection of this freedom by labor and management and of a substantial degree of public assent to its continuance.

While the factors which govern the conduct of the parties and of their negotiators in conflict situations vary widely and are obviously at times of a very different qualitative order, the human subject matter on which these factors play, and the emotions which they stimulate, bear the inescapable marks of a common humanity. We would suggest that any parallels between the two areas of mediation experience by no means need to rest entirely, or even principally, on the comparability of the institutional settings or on an item-by-item matching of the power variables.

Our analysis suggests the following as the principal reasons why parallels exist in mediation experience in the two fields of conflict:

1. Disputes occur between powerfully organized groups which have managed to preserve considerable freedom of action.
2. The conflicts touch what each organized group believes to be matters of vital interest—occasionally these matters are believed to relate to group survival.
3. The large majority of disputes in both fields involve the balance of power between the conflicting parties.
4. In each field the future status of the negotiators is frequently

dependent upon the degree to which they can achieve the initially outlined goals.

5. In both fields there is a growing realization of the economic and the human cost of conflict. In many cases this is accompanied by a growing assent to the use of governmental or intergovernmental machinery designed to assist the reaching of agreement.

6. Conflicts in both areas are usually accompanied by strong emotional overtones, and the reduction of individual and group emotion is at least partially a problem in human relations, as well as being a problem in substantive settlement.

### Arrangements Which Appear to Facilitate a Settlement

It is apparent from the discussion of the two fields that somewhat similar general problems are encountered. The need to initiate mediation in such a way that the parties in conflict have maximum confidence in the mediatory arrangements and personnel, the degree of flexibility which should be permitted the mediator and the parties in seeking and arriving at a settlement, the usefulness of avoiding extended public debate, these are questions which appear to arise in any mediatory effort. The differing institutional settings may dictate differing approaches. On the other hand there may be certain general principles which can be isolated, based on the general response of individuals and groups in conflict situations.

While it is clear from our analysis that as disputes approach mediation there are certain similarities in the manner in which they are handled, the most direct similarities appear to lie in the techniques used by mediators once the disputes are submitted to mediation. We will discuss first the general relationship of the parties to the public mediation agency and the manner in which the dispute is brought into mediation, and then turn to the question of techniques. We will put forward a series of tentative conclusions. By reference to the experience in the labor and international fields we will attempt to indicate the general validity and the limitations of each conclusion.

## ADAPTING THE MEDIATORY MACHINERY TO THE PARTICULAR DISPUTE

*In each dispute there is a need to adapt the mediatory machinery to the special circumstances of the particular case. This applies both to the type of special machinery created to handle the dispute and to the personnel chosen for the mediatory task. Consultation with the parties is usually an aid to the creation of the machinery and the selection of the personnel most likely to prove successful.*

While the Security Council and the General Assembly in their peacemaking functions serve in general as international mediation boards, they usually attempt promptly to devise a subsidiary body to which they can entrust the more detailed mediation effort. In those cases in which the President or other persons in a position to use their good offices have attempted private discussions, these have frequently proved helpful in determining the type of special mediatory effort which might be undertaken. In two cases substantive progress was made in such discussions toward a settlement, but to date there has been no instance in which such discussions have in themselves been sufficient to bring final agreement.

Each dispute that comes to the United Nations has its own peculiarities, based on the type of situation from which it springs, the characteristics of the parties in conflict, and the history of the dispute. We have described the different types of subsidiary bodies which have been created by the Security Council or by the General Assembly to conduct the continuing and more detailed negotiations. The special instrument created must be one which will carry the general confidence of the parent organ. It should

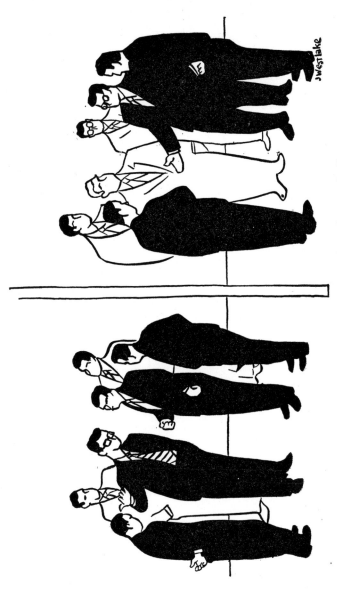

The mediatory machinery must be adapted to each dispute.

127

be a sturdy symbol of the international public concern for the peaceful settlement of the dispute. If it is to be effective it must be one which has initially, or can gain, a substantial measure of the confidence of the parties in conflict.

It is easy to see why, as the mediation process was becoming established in the United Nations, governments were so frequently appointed as members of the conciliation commissions. Their presence, as governments, on the commissions was believed to give these commissions a certain stability and firmness and a general support which would assist them in gaining the respect of the parties in conflict. It meant that the commissions could not easily be ignored. In cases in which such commissions were appointed one might say that the mediation machinery was being adapted first to the need to enhance the general authority of the United Nations in its intervention in the dispute, and more particularly to give prestige and authority to the special mediatory agent established to conduct the negotiations. In the governments appointed, and in those governments' selection of their representatives, an adaptation was then attempted to the other circumstances of the dispute and to the special interests and concerns of the parties.

This approach may have been a useful one in the early stages of the United Nations attempt to establish in practice a right to intervene which had been established in principle in the Charter. Such "instructed commissions," however, have demonstrated certain limitations in flexibility and effectiveness. The United Nations is already experimenting progressively with other types of subsidiary bodies. In any organization, in the long run, it is the results which build prestige. The United Nations may have reached the stage in its handling of disputes where, in the creation of the subsidiary body, it can now give its attention not so much to the political authority of that body, but as to how it can be so devised as to include the necessary experience and political judgment, how it can have the necessary flexibility, and how it can begin its activities with the maximum confidence of the parties in its impartiality and competence.

A symbol of respect has often been utilized to gain confidence in labor mediation. In India, for example, high court judges are used almost exclusively. In Sweden governors of provinces have often been used; in fact successful mediators are often appointed to such posts as a means of enhancing their prestige and keeping their mediatory services available. In the early history of mediation in the United States efforts were made to associate an institutional respect with the peacemaking effort. An evolution has taken place in the United States, however, toward the use of individuals with both a reputation for impartiality and with special skills. This would appear to have been a useful development.

We have suggested that in both labor and international disputes the special mediatory effort is frequently formulated in consultation with the parties. In the case of the Committee of Good Offices, the Netherlands and the Indonesian Republican government each nominated a government to sit on the Committee and these two selected a third. In the creation of other commissions background consultations have taken place previous to the appointment of member governments. If the United Nations should try out the effectiveness of "uninstructed" commissions, consultation with the parties on personnel, previous to appointment, would be even more useful—for in this case it would be the selection of the individuals who would inspire confidence in their conduct of the mediation effort that would be in question, and not just the selection of governments who would then make their own designations of personnel.

It would be difficult, if not impossible, for a single mediator, who was distrusted by one of the parties, to carry out any useful function. Conversely, if the parties have agreed to a single mediator, it is somewhat more difficult for them later to reject his efforts. The same principles would apply in the selection and work of a commission. We have noted the tripartite nature of the Committee of Good Offices in the Indonesian dispute. In setting up the first Commission on India and Pakistan the United Nations attempted to establish it on a similar principle. India selected Czechoslovakia and Pakistan selected Argentina. After continued failure of the countries to agree on the selection of a third country, the Security Council expanded the Commission by the addition of Belgium and Colombia and the President of the Council appointed the United States as fifth member.

While other United Nations commissions have not been established so clearly on a tripartite basis, the effort has frequently been made, in consultation with the parties in conflict, to include as members of the commission one or more states which are believed by each disputant to be sympathetic with, or to have an especially good understanding of, their problems and point of view. While this places a somewhat heavier burden on the other neutral or impartial members and occasionally creates internal problems for the commission, it does frequently contribute to the parties' willingness to have the commission undertake mediation.

Full consultation with the parties in the initial handling of the dispute by the parent body is more, however, than merely a means of discovering the type of subsidiary body most likely to be effective and launching it with some initial confidence of the disputants that it will be useful and impartial. We have suggested that the political organs of the United Nations, in their handling of international disputes, serve as international mediation boards. From the time they accept jurisdiction in a dispute their principal effort should be to prepare the way for a settlement. The mediation process has already begun. Thus the whole pattern of discussion in the parent organ, and the negotiations undertaken with the parties on its behalf, should be such as to build the confidence of the disputants in its impartiality and in the appropriateness of its concerning itself with a settlement of the dispute. Frequently the parties recognize the legitimacy, or even the necessity, of United Nations intervention, but as has been pointed out, one or both of them may resent the fact of such intervention. In the "feeling-out process" which is undertaken by the state bringing the dispute or situation to the attention of the United Nations, or by the sponsors of the resolution setting up the special mediatory machinery, or in any informal conversation undertaken by the President of the Security Council or of the General Assembly, some of this resentment can be relieved and the parties given the feeling that their special circumstances will be understood and proper attention will be given them.

In labor conflicts the use of single mediators, of several associated mediators, and of mediating and fact-finding commissions has developed out of a vast amount of experience in conflicts of varying intensities. The selection of a single mediator in such disputes is obviously considerably easier than it is in the international field. Over a period of years certain individuals have gained experience in some one section of industrial life. The fact that they and their previous work are known, makes an agreement for the use of their services a much simpler process. While familiarity with an industry is usually an aid in getting a mediation effort under way promptly, governmental mediation agencies are careful not to push the principle of specialization too far. A broad experience usually adds to the effectiveness of a mediator.

We have noted that the mediation agreements established by the Railway Labor Act and those set up to handle disputes in the

United States atomic-energy plants were developed out of extensive consultation with management and the unions. It seems likely that some of the subsequent success of both of these patterns of settlement has been due to the full consultations which preceded their creation.

Similarly, virtually all machinery developed in the United States for settling special labor disputes during the Second World War and in the present emergency has not only been devised in consultation with management and labor, but has been established on a tripartite basis. Since the War Labor Board, created in the Second World War, proved to be one of the most effective emergency arrangements for the settlement of labor disputes that has been developed in the United States, it may be worth noting the manner in which it was formed.

At a labor-management conference held in December, 1941, the unions and management which were represented agreed to follow a no-strike-no-lockout policy for the war period. The Executive Order creating the War Labor Board, by agreement of representatives of labor and management, therefore provided "that for the duration of the war there shall be no strikes or lockouts and that all labor disputes shall be settled by peaceful means." The Board became the custodian of the December agreement and was given initial powers which possibly could most aptly be described as those of voluntary arbitration. The decisions of the Board, however, were still recommendations to the parties to the dispute and the Board had a compliance problem. Some unions contended they had not been a party to the no-strike-no-lockout agreement. If the recommendations were rejected and a work stoppage occurred, the government usually seized the plant while the Board continued its efforts to get the parties to acquiesce in its decision. Under the pressure of the national emergency this usually proved sufficient.

The powers of the Board were somewhat reinforced in July, 1943, with the passage of the War Labor Disputes Act, but these powers still derived fundamentally from the no-strike-no-lockout agreement of December, 1941.[1] The fact that labor and management were partners with the government in the development of plans for the War Labor Board, the fact that it was tripartite and that either could withdraw from it, if it took or was about to take some action of which either of them strongly disapproved, made them willing to give up temporarily an independence of action the relinquishment of which would otherwise have been most repugnant to them. The Board had an excellent compliance record. Out of 17,807 disputes handled, involving 12,300,000 employees, there were only 51 cases in which the parties refused to accept the Board's decision.

These experiences in the handling of labor disputes suggest the great advantages of all potential disputants, or of those who represent them, feeling that they have had some part, even though small, in the creation or the development of any standing governmental agency charged with responsibility for mediation.

### THE ROLE AND LIMITATIONS OF PUBLIC DEBATE

*Public debate of the issues in dispute is occasionally an aid in the mobilization of the public interest for peaceful settlement. Extended public debate by the parties in conflict tends, however, to harden them in their respective points of view.*

Once an international dispute is placed on the agenda of the Security Council or the General Assembly, if a special investi-

---

[1]This was made abundantly clear by the refusal of both labor and management, at the termination of the war, to permit the continuance of this type of arrangement for "peaceful settlement" of their disputes. This refusal was the forerunner of the large number of labor disputes in the reconversion period.

gating commission is not needed, the first step has usually been a public debate in which the parties state their positions and outline what seems to them to be the nature of the dispute. This process enables each party to test out its case and its bargaining positions vis-à-vis the other party and in relation to the other countries around the Council table or in the General Assembly.

Although it can hardly be said that the general debate which has usually followed the opening statements by the parties provides an accurate barometer of the degree to which an "international public interest" exists for peaceful settlement of a dispute, it usually does illustrate the degree to which this concern is present in those governmental circles in a position to effect a settlement. It can also be an important factor in the stimulation of additional constructive international concern. It thus is an aid in the creation of a public "power factor" which must be taken into account by the disputants. In an international organization such as the United Nations, which has been charged by its Members with the peaceful settlement of international disputes, but whose intervention on behalf of the public interest in any particular dispute is likely to be viewed with substantial misgivings by one or both parties to the conflict, the importance of this process must not be overlooked.

At the same time it is clear that extended public debate in the United Nations is capable of making a conflict more difficult of solution. This is especially the case if the parties to the dispute, in their presentations, take extreme positions not previously taken in public, if their respective positions in the dispute are hardened through repetition, or if the occasion is used to engage in public recriminations. It might thus be said that while public debate of international disputes may occasionally be necessary as a means of building up the power of the United Nations to deal with certain difficult disputes, it is frequently a questionable and risky substitute for a more willing and confident acceptance by the member states of less formal and less publicized United Nations mediatory efforts. It is possible that, as the organization demonstrates progressively its impartiality and competence, member states will more frequently permit it to take a mediatory initiative without the necessity of such formal arraignment of a case before the Security Council or the General Assembly. We

While public debate occasionally stimulates public support for a mediated settlement, prolonged debate hardens the parties in their positions.

might note in this connection the experience in the League of Nations minorities system. After starting out with the premise that public discussion of minority issues would be a useful thing, it was found in many cases that discussion had aggravated the situation and had not been an aid to an effective solution.

In the chapter on the handling of international disputes we have referred to the resolution passed by the Security Council, drawing on League experience in using a rapporteur, and suggested that there was a growing tendency in the United Nations for the President of the Security Council or the President of the General Assembly to hold private conferences with the parties in an effort to help them find a solution or to discover the way in which the political organ could most effectively promote a settlement.[2] It would appear, thus, that the United Nations is already experimenting with other patterns of initial consideration which would avoid the difficulties inherent in extended public debate. Special efforts in this respect were made by General Mac-Naughton of Canada in the Kashmir dispute when he held the Presidency of the Security Council and by Mr. Bramuglia of the Argentine in the Berlin dispute when he held the same position. In both cases a great deal of initiative was taken. The General Assembly has similarly made use of its President in the Greek dispute in the fall of 1948 (Dr. Evatt) and in the Korean conflict in the fall and winter of 1950–1951 (Mr. Entezam). In the former case, the Secretary-General was one of those associated with the President in the mediation effort. Further experimentation may indicate that the public debate is less necessary than was originally supposed as a means of demonstrating international concern for peaceful settlement, and may suggest that other means can be developed for getting the facts concerning the dispute, for stimulating public support for peaceful settlement, and for gaining some general indication of the type of settlement for which there would be substantial international support.

In the early history of labor disputes the conflicting parties

[2]In his statement to the Council at the time the above resolution was presented, Ambassador Gross, representing the United States, called attention to the parallels in labor experience.

often took their cases to the public in an effort to gain support. They still do frequently in the more stubborn conflicts. Such action is usually taken, however, outside the framework of mediation and is rarely if ever encouraged or fostered by the mediator or the mediating agency. Quite the opposite is the case. The Federal Mediation and Conciliation Service in the United States feels so strongly about the adverse effect of such public discussion that they advise the disputants, when the Service intervenes, to avoid any discussion of the case with representatives of the press during the mediation effort.

There may be occasions in which unions or management have taken their cases to the public and, finding little support for their positions, have then been more willing to compromise, but there are probably a much larger number of cases in which one or the other party, being convinced of the rightness of its point of view, believes it has stirred additional support and is thus less willing to modify its position. Having gone "on record" before the public, retreat is then more difficult.

### PROPER TIMING OF THE MEDIATION EFFORT

*In a mediation effort in which the power of the conflicting parties is not grossly unequal, agreement between them is likely to be achieved at the time when they are both least rigid in their positions. This may be early in the dispute before their public positions have hardened, or it may be at some later time when the disputants are most conscious of the risks inherent in a failure to agree.*

In the mediation of both labor and international disputes, the timing of the mediator's intervention is of considerable importance. The results of a mediator using identical approaches at two different periods in the history of a dispute are likely to be very different.

The timing of intervention must take account of many variables, some of which may apply only to the particular dispute. In the great majority of conflicts, the rigidity with which the negotiators will cling to their positions will vary, depending upon the impact of the counterarguments, the assessment of their bargaining strength, their ability vis-à-vis their constituents to alter an announced goal, and perhaps most important, a full realization of the consequences of open conflict. The rigidity may be great

Successful mediation depends upon the parties in conflict being able to retreat from extreme or untenable positions.

at the initiation of direct negotiations, it may again hit a peak during the course of the negotiations, and then taper off, or it may be greatest just before the parties decide to break off their conferences. There is no rule of thumb which will predict these fluctuations. Other things being equal a mediation effort is likely to achieve success at a time when both sides show some willingness to depart from any rigid positions previously assumed. This may be early in the dispute when both parties have reached a deadlock in direct negotiations and before they have "taken their case to the public," or it may be at a later stage when both are weary of argument and are viewing with apprehension the consequences of a failure to reach a settlement.

In the absence of an intimate knowledge of the conflict and of the factors which are playing upon it, or of an opportunity for informal talks with the parties, it is not easy to judge the amenability of a dispute to the process of mediation. The tone of public utterances of the negotiators may represent an effort to create bargaining strength and may have no relationship to their real willingness to compromise. Occasionally the parties will issue their most extreme statements before their first negotiating conference is held. Nevertheless, while the willingness to compromise may not be accurately reflected by the speeches made, once public statements are made they become part of the background, conditioning and sometimes restricting the future action of the negotiator and his constituents. Retreat from extreme positions publicly taken may not be easy. For this reason it is frequently an advantage for the mediation effort to be initiated before public statements have been made.

In some disputes the dangers inherent in a failure to agree are relatively inconsequential. The conflict may continue without serious damage to either party for a considerable period of time. In other disputes the relationship between the parties is such that a failure to gain a settlement will have major adverse economic or political consequences for one or both of them. In disputes in which the hazards of a failure to agree are progressively apparent and of approximately equal import to both parties, the rigidity in the positions of both may be least as a speed-up takes place in the preparations for battle.

We would not conclude from this, however, that the mediator should necessarily wait until this moment to enter the dispute. His ability to gain a last-minute settlement may well be based on his knowledge of the parties, of their positions, and of the background of the conflict, and on the parties' confidence in him, largely or entirely acquired through his previous efforts at settlement. Such a last-minute compromise may also be facilitated by the pressure of public opinion or of groups not a party to the dispute, whose interest in the mediation effort has developed over several months until it has become a formidable force in support of a mediated settlement.

The majority of international disputes have a long history and few of them have been submitted to the United Nations promptly enough to permit much discretion in the decision as to the time of intervention. The theory of the Charter is that the parties shall settle their disputes peacefully by means of their own choice. They are legally obligated not to resort to force. We have noted that in many cases it is not until a continuing deadlock has deteriorated into open conflict that the dispute is brought formally to the attention of the Security Council or the General Assembly and its intervention is requested.

There is no reason for assuming it was the intention of the drafters of the Charter that the two political organs should not concern themselves with disputes previous to their reaching a crisis or erupting into military conflict. But the limited powers which the United Nations was given and the slowness with which governments have acknowledged the appropriateness, and frequently the necessity, of its mediatory intervention in international disputes have led the Members of the United Nations to put the initial emphasis on the peaceful settlement of those disputes which have clearly developed to the point where they "threaten international peace and security." It is always a matter of judgment, however, as to whether any particular deadlocked dispute has become, or is likely to become, a threat to the peace. At times it is possibly somewhat easier for third parties close to the dispute to ascertain the fact than it is under the existing circumstances for any state or for the Secretary-General to reach the decision to request United Nations intervention. The serious nature of such a move militates against prompt action. As we have suggested, there is the implied accusation that one or both parties are threatening the peace. There may be claims of "domestic jurisdiction" or claims that the actions taken are proper under the Charter as measures of self-defense. Thus, unless a move to request consideration by the United Nations is for propaganda purposes, it is usually a sober and considered decision and is frequently not taken until the dispute has substantially disturbed other sections of the international community.

Although at a much lower place on the "conflict scale," the early experience in labor mediation was not unlike that through which the United Nations is now passing. It was not until industrial disputes had disturbed the larger community that governmental mediation efforts were undertaken. They were then instituted in an effort to protect the "public interest." It has been only as the unions, and especially as management, gained some measure of confidence in governmental efforts and came more nearly to accept the appropriateness of government intervention, that these efforts could move progressively toward an earlier intervention in the dispute.

The appropriateness of governmental mediatory intervention in labor disputes is still not acknowledged in some sections of American industrial life. Management and representatives of unions still occasionally emphasize with some vehemence that they "don't need outsiders trying to settle our problems." The entrance of a governmental mediator is still frequently looked upon by management or the union as a mark of failure. The general acceptability of governmental intervention has developed to the point, however, where it was written into the Taft-Hartley Act that the Federal Mediation and Conciliation Service, and any state mediation service in whose territory the industry is located, should be notified 30 days in advance of the termination of contracts. In Sweden an even longer notification is given.

While in the United States these notifications do not always take place, the procedure has in general simplified the approach of the public mediatory agencies in the labor field to the delicate question of their possible intervention in the dispute. On the basis of the formal notification they can concern themselves with the conflict situation previous to the expiration of a contract and before a strike is called. The provision has not entirely eliminated, but it has somewhat lessened, the awkwardness which frequently prevailed earlier as to whether one of the parties would request the intervention of the public agency or whether the agency would intervene on its own responsibility. The act of notification is not only a reminder to the parties of a possible public interest in any results which might flow from the continuance of the dispute, but it is one additional step toward a general acknowledgment of the appropriateness of possible governmental mediatory intervention as an expression of the public interest.

There is a great difference between the circumstances under which labor mediation is now undertaken in the national community and the development and present treatment of an international dispute in the world community. The intervention of the mediatory agency in a labor dispute is clearly on a much more informal basis than is the intervention of either the Security Council or the General Assembly. Governmental mediation agencies have the power to enter the dispute on the basis of an administrative decision if they conclude that their mediatory efforts might be useful and if they believe it is a matter in which they have jurisdiction. This gives a freedom in the timing which is far different from the formal and quasi-legislative considerations in the United Nations. It permits the mediatory agency to enter the case without any great publicity. In the United States it represents a great advance in the acceptance of public mediation efforts in the 37-year period since Secretary Wilson used with such caution the mediatory powers given him when the U.S. Department of Labor was established.

It is frequently assumed that a national mediatory agency has little difficulty in a labor dispute in deciding whether or not it should enter the case. It is true that in the vast majority of dispute situations the administrative decision is taken promptly on the basis of discussions with the parties and of personal knowledge of the industry and of its general relationship to the public welfare. However, with the increasing interdependence of the national economy, and with the development of nation-wide unions and trade associations, a small dispute in one section of industry may quickly become a complex and urgent matter of national interest. The decision for a governmental body to enter the case is thus frequently not a simple one.

There are certain similarities in the two fields in the equally liberal interpretations given of the jurisdiction of the mediatory agency. In both cases, if there is evidence of exhaustion of efforts to reach a direct settlement between the parties and if the dispute appears within the agency's general jurisdiction, it usually decides to take the case. If the facts or the nature of the dispute are unclear, the mediatory body frequently sends out representatives to make a special investigation. In labor disputes the investigator is usually an individual; in international disputes a commission is more frequently sent.

The continuing emphasis on national sovereignty and the uncertainty on the part of member states as to the proper limitations on their own, or their competitor's, freedom of action combine to make states reluctant to see United Nations intervention in disputes to which they are a party or to see precedents set which might later prove embarrassing to them. It would nevertheless be reasonable to suppose that if the United Nations is able to demonstrate, progressively, its ability with wisdom and effectiveness to cope with the disputes that come before it, a willingness may slowly develop for it to extend its good offices and its mediatory efforts before the positions of the parties become so firmly fixed and their activities have an opportunity so seriously to threaten the international peace.

We might note in this connection the freedom given the General Assembly in the Charter to discuss "any questions or any matters within the scope of the present Charter" (Article 10) and to "discuss any questions relating to the maintenance of international peace and security" (Article 11). The responsibilities of the Security Council and the General Assembly are clearly stated, to consider not only disputes which endanger the peace but also "situations" deemed likely to impair the general welfare or friendly relations among nations.

It is not difficult to see the wisdom of the United Nations refraining from bringing a large number of these situations into debate in the General Assembly or the Security Council. While either organ might occasionally concern itself with indirect action designed to lessen the tension, direct debate might be resisted on the grounds that the issues lie within the domestic jurisdiction of the parties. Such public debate might in fact serve to aggravate the situation. A further complication is the difficulty in some situations of determining the respective interests of the several states that may be involved. If the aggravating issues continue and the situation develops into a full-fledged dispute this becomes much clearer. In the earlier stages concerned states may not themselves have determined their respective interests.

Public debate, however, is not the only choice open to the United Nations. At several points in this study we have suggested the steady development of more informal methods in the initial mediation activities of the United Nations. These have centered primarily around the President of the Security Council, the President of the General Assembly, or individuals or small groups appointed by them. A somewhat different type of negotiation was undertaken by the Secretary-General in connection with his ten-point program. It is at least conceivable, now that the responsibility of the General Assembly has been increased, that the Presidents of the General Assembly and of the Security Council might occasionally be requested to use their good offices in disputes before these conflicts are brought formally before one of the political organs.

Another possibility would be a development in the negotiation which now takes place before a member state or the Secretary-General decides to bring a dispute to the attention of the Council or of the Assembly. The Labor Relations Panel in the United States atomic-energy plants occasionally sends an advance representative to investigate a dispute as an aid in determining whether or not the agency should enter the case. At times the investigation and work of these advance representatives has aided the parties in breaking an initial deadlock and resolving the dispute. It is unlikely in international tension or dispute situations that similar investigation or good offices work would have parallel results, but, if carried out with wisdom and inventiveness in the early stages of a dispute, it might be instrumental to the discovery of less formal means of treatment which would facilitate settlement and which would avoid the arraignment and debate of the dispute before the Security Council or the General Assembly.

### THE NEED FOR FLEXIBILITY IN THE MEDIATION EFFORT

*A mediation effort is usually less difficult if it can operate within broad terms of reference and with a maximum of internal flexibility. This suggests the general desirability in conflicts in which the emphasis is on mediating a settlement, of using uninstructed single mediators.*

There are times when for political or other reasons it is impossible to give certain difficult mediation efforts flexible terms of reference. Experience in labor disputes would strongly suggest, however, that in the hands of skilled negotiators a wide area of discretion is usually an aid to settlement. The mediator may reject certain seemingly extraneous issues presented by the parties after giving these issues attention, but the mediation effort is frequently handicapped if questions believed by one of the parties to be relevant to the case are excluded entirely from consideration.

Labor mediators usually have a great deal of freedom in the manner in which they operate. One of the best illustrations is the work of the U.S. Atomic Energy Labor Relations Panel. In this area of potential labor-management conflict, as in no other, the United States government might have been expected to give way to the temptation to prescribe rigid arrangements for settlement or to establish some form of compulsory arbitration. In the chapter dealing with the handling of labor disputes in the United States we have indicated the extreme flexibility of the mediation arrangements finally established and the general success of the Labor Relations Panel.

In the international field the experience is less conclusive, but it would appear to be developing along similar lines. We have noted the effective use made by the late Count Bernadotte and by Ralph Bunche of the comprehensive terms of reference given them in the Palestine conflict. It was only as the initial mediation effort in Indonesia won for itself broader terms of reference and especially the freedom to make suggestions and initiate proposals that it was able to make substantial progress in settling the conflict.

The only exception to this need for flexible terms of reference would likely be a situation in which one of the parties was much the weaker and the clearly obvious justice of its cause called for supporting terms of reference by the Security Council or the General Assembly.

In our first tentative conclusion we suggested that different types of conflict situations required different types of mediatory commissions and that it was important, in each dispute, to find the one best suited to the situation. The answer might be a single mediator, it might be a commission composed of three or more individuals, or it might be a commission composed of three or more governments, called an "instructed commission." Some trend can be noted in the United Nations toward the use of single mediators. Count Bernadotte and Ralph Bunche in Palestine and Sir Owen Dixon in Kashmir are examples. We have also referred to the development of the United Nations Panel on Inquiry and Conciliation and its use in connection with Dr. Graham's appointment in April, 1951, as United Nations Representative for India and Pakistan.

Governmental commissions are by their very nature more cumbersome in operation. To the problem of harmonizing the approaches of the three or five persons serving on the commission and finding a basis for reconciling the parties in dispute is added, in such cases, the problem of the adjustment of the divergent approaches of the appointing governments. The merits of the case as seen from the vantage point of direct negotiations with the parties in dispute may be different from the merits as

viewed from the various national capitals. Substantial time is
often required in reporting conversations to home governments,
in getting replies, and in attempting to harmonize these replies
before going on to the next stage in negotiation with the parties.
Such an approach scarcely makes for speed, flexibility, and
effectiveness.

In contrast, a single mediator in consultation with his staff
can adjust promptly to the developing factors in the case and
move quickly from discussion with one party to discussion with
the other, concerned only with an agreement acceptable to the
parties and not out of keeping with what he believes to be the
public interest.

It is for these reasons that the United Nations has begun to
give greater attention to the use of a single mediator. For similar
reasons initial mediation efforts in labor conflicts are customarily
undertaken by single mediators. It is usually only after such
initial efforts in labor conflicts have failed and a greater threat
to the public interest develops that resort is made to some other
form of mediation—most frequently some type of commission.
This would suggest that a single mediator is likely to be more
suitable in those disputes which have not developed to the point
where it is necessary to bring to bear, or to mobilize and then
bring to focus, the full force of public opinion in an effort to get
the parties in conflict to abandon incompatible goals or those
believed to be inimical to the general public interest. Under the
following heading we will suggest some reasons why the work of
Count Bernadotte and Ralph Bunche in Palestine does not appear
to be an invalidating exception.

### PUBLIC REPORTS AND RECOMMENDATIONS

*In major conflicts in which the mediating and reporting functions
are likely to be combined and in which a report, with recom-*

Single mediators can move with more speed and flexibility.

*mendations for settlement, is likely to be made to a superior body or the public, there are frequently distinct advantages in the appointment of a commission instead of a single mediator. In international disputes this can be a commission composed either of outstanding individuals or of governments.*

Reference has been made to the use in public-emergency labor disputes of fact-finding commissions which have combined the mediating and reporting function. Some of these commissions have been free to make recommendations. We have noted in these cases the large number of times in which the eventual settlement was in line with the recommendations of the commission.

One essential power of such a commission comes from its potential ability, through its report, to deflate publicly the exaggerated claims of the parties in conflict. This is an especially important consideration for industries which are dependent upon public good will. For a commission to have the power of making public a recommendation for settlement, based on its study of the merits of the case, is an even more potent lever. What these commissions lose in flexibility from having three or five members they usually make up for through the added prestige which comes from having the report made by a group. Other things being equal it would appear to be human nature to give greater weight to the carefully considered and united conclusions of a group of impartial and able persons than to the considered judgment of one equally qualified person.

The same general approach would seem to apply to a report to a superior body in an international dispute. Because the majority of disputes which come before the United Nations have reached such a serious stage before mediation is undertaken, it has usually been essential for the United Nations to give even more attention than is given in labor disputes to the authority and

prestige of the fact-finding or mediating commissions. In our discussion of the adaptation of the subsidiary mediation machinery
to the particular dispute we have noted that one of the reasons
for the use by the United Nations of "instructed commissions"
was the belief that governmental membership would enhance
the authority and prestige of such a commission. Since the large

When the emphasis is on marshaling public support for peaceful
settlement, a report from a mediation board is likely to carry more
weight.

majority of United Nations commissions have combined the mediating and reporting functions and since under this present heading we are dealing with those factors which add to a commission's general prestige, it might be useful if we considered more thoroughly this suggestion with regard to instructed commissions.

Three arguments are frequently advanced for the appointment of instructed commissions.

1. It is believed that governmental membership would enhance the authority and prestige of a commission in its mediatory, but especially in its reporting functions.

There is no simple formula for building the prestige of a commission. Let us look, for example, at one of the more successful United Nations mediation efforts—that in Indonesia. The work of the initial Good Offices Committee was undoubtedly facilitated by the fact that governments were represented on the tripartite committee. This was an important factor in demonstrating the concern with which the international community viewed the conflict and in the Committee being permitted to undertake its work. The reports to the Security Council gained in prestige by having on them the stamp of approval of the three governments (United States, Australia, Belgium). The fact that it was tripartite probably gave it an added weight with the parties in conflict.

On the other hand some of the success of the Good Offices Committee and of the subsequent Commission on Indonesia stemmed out of the work of the third member, first Frank Graham and then Merle Cochran. While the work of these men was enhanced by the fact that each of them represented the United States, the United States government, because of its confidence in them, may have permitted them a freedom in negotiation which enabled them to operate as members of a tripartite commission with a flexibility very similar to that of a single mediator. Governmental representation added something but the quality and competence of the personnel was such as to set the stage for this added element.

Governmental prestige can seldom make up for, or rescue, a poor performance on the part of a governmental representative. If an unsuitable person represents a government, that may be a severely complicating element detracting not only from the commission's competence in its work but also from the prestige of its report. One might raise the question as to whether the experience of United Nations commissions did not suggest that the quality and suitability of personnel was not of first importance in the establishment of a commission's general effectiveness. With governmental membership there is always the possibility that an unsuitable person will be replaced. Such replacements, however, have seldom taken place.

2. The case has often been made for United Nations commissions composed of governments on the ground that they made possible a type of background diplomatic support to the mediation effort, while it is in process, which would not otherwise be likely. In certain situations this may have been true. Without a much more complete analysis of United Nations mediation experience it would be difficult to judge the extent to which this background activity has been an aid to settlement and the extent to which it may, at times, have been a complicating factor. In view of the vigorous diplomatic support which Count Bernadotte and Ralph Bunche were able to command in their work in Palestine it could scarcely be maintained, however, that governmental membership on commissions was an essential prerequisite to the giving of substantial diplomatic support to a mediation effort.

3. A third reason suggested for the appointment of governments to commissions is that it thus becomes possible to include

within the framework of the special mediation effort several of the divergent approaches present in the Security Council or the General Assembly. Occasionally it is only on such terms that the Council or the Assembly is able to gain sufficient agreement to pass the resolution establishing a subsidiary mediatory organ. This may sometimes take the extreme form of one group of states refusing to vote in favor of a resolution unless some provision is made for regional representation in the proposed commission.

To the extent that the inclusion of the principal divergent interests is necessitated as a means of getting any subsidiary machinery established which can carry forward a mediation effort, it may at times be justified. Such a commission may be a distinct advance over any of the other measures for settlement available. It may still be possible for such a commission to present a report if a settlement is not achieved. While circumstances may dictate such an approach, it would appear to be a somewhat precarious basis for an effective mediation effort. We might note in this connection, that it usually requires a fairly cohesive approach on the part of the Security Council for the appointment of a single mediator. The type of approach we have been discussing above lies at the other end of the scale.

Under this general heading we have been concerned with the extent to which the presence of governments on United Nations commissions contributed to the prestige, authority, and effectiveness of mediation and reporting efforts. We have noted the importance which must be attached, even in these situations, to qualified personnel. Other considerations may in the end determine the best type of mediation machinery to be established but all types depend for their success on the person or persons selected. This central importance of personnel would suggest that the United Nations might do well to give further consideration to the means of ensuring a high level of appointment.

In our discussion of the handling of labor disputes we have set out what would appear to be useful qualities for those undertaking labor mediation. The qualifications of a good mediator in the international field would appear to be very similar. While eminence is an attribute which may enhance the initial prestige of a mediator or commission, certain other qualities may contribute equally to success. Humility, tact, and patience are three such qualities. One important guide in the selection of suitable personnel is likely to be an already demonstrated success in the field of human relations.

It was the practice under the League of Nations for nominations by governments for conciliation work to be discussed with the Secretary-General before being presented to the League Council. This helped to ensure the useful balancing of skills and experience in the mediation effort. This practice might be further developed in the United Nations at times when governmental appointments to instructed commissions are pending.

But instructed commissions are not the only alternative in the United Nations to single mediators. Experience in labor mediation would indicate that commissions composed of three or more qualified individuals, appointed in a personal capacity, may at certain times have advantages over a single mediator. In serious conflicts in the international field such commissions might have more capacity to enlist the support of international public opinion behind their report to the Security Council or to the General Assembly, or their recommendations for settlement, than would a single mediator. The greater geographical representation in the commission might in itself be an important factor in enlisting this interest. At the same time they could be expected to have more flexibility in their mediation work prior to a report than would a commission composed of governments. Personnel for such commissions might be drawn from the United Nations Panel on Inquiry and Conciliation or from other sources. It could be nominated by an especially created Nominations Committee, by the sponsors of the resolution creating the proposed commission, or by the President of the Security Council or the General Assembly, depending upon which body was dealing with the dispute.

To date the United Nations has not experimented to any great extent with commissions of three or more qualified persons appointed as individuals. In the spring of 1947 Ambassador Austin of the United States Mission to the United Nations proposed such a commission in connection with the Greek border dispute. In the Korean conflict Mr. Entezam, President of the General Assembly, Sir Benegal Rau of India, and Mr. Lester Pearson of Canada were asked to use their good offices in an effort to discover possible terms of settlement. Subsequently, Mr. Entezam was asked to associate with himself a committee which would continue the effort to arrange a satisfactory cease-fire in Korea. He selected Mr. Grafstrom of Sweden and Mr. Nervo of Mexico. In both the first and second committees the selections would appear to be related not only to the very substantial personal qualifications of the persons chosen, but also to their prominent connection with the policies pursued by their respective governments and to a recognition of the importance of regional representation. Thus while the Good Offices Committee technically retained its independence, the selections were made with reference to some of the same background factors that usually lie behind appointments to United Nations instructed or governmental commissions. Because of the prominent positions held by the men it was not likely that they would depart far from the policies of their respective governments. In the case of Sir Benegal Rau and Mr. Grafstrom the facilities of their governments in Peking were considered to be an asset in the negotiations.

The use of this type of commission deserves further exploration. The general approach may represent a very useful half step toward uninstructed commissions under circumstances which permit flexibility in selection and in operation, while retaining some of the authority and prestige elements previously associated with instructed or governmental commissions.

## Similarities in Negotiation Techniques

We turn now to some of the similarities in mediation techniques which have emerged from our considerations.

### TECHNIQUES IN GETTING AGREEMENT

*The techniques for getting agreement between the parties to a dispute, once it has been submitted to mediation, are very similar in the international and in the labor fields. Wide latitude must be left, however, for the mediator's own personal approach and sense of timing.*

**Getting the parties together.** One of the mediator's first responsibilities in any type of dispute is to determine whether he should attempt to get the parties together and, if so, under what circumstances. In both labor and international disputes emotions are usually well stirred by the time mediation is undertaken. We have suggested that in labor disputes the parties are frequently brought together first to consider less controversial subjects such as the general procedure for the conduct of the negotiations. Sir Frederick Leggett, in his chapter on British mediation experience, has referred to the dispute affecting the cotton industry in 1932. Here the parties, who were in a very firm state of mind with regard to their positions, were first brought together to discuss a new permanent conciliation machinery and to see if agreement could be reached on the principles

The steps through which a mediation effort moves, once it is launched, are very similar in the labor and international fields.

which should govern the observance of collective agreements. In Sweden, the initial discussion often touches on some of the general background factors lying behind the particular points in conflict. It is usually only after the mediator has discussed with the parties the possibility of an initial meeting, or at times only after such a meeting has taken place, that he can judge the extent to which the mediation effort should be conducted with the parties remaining separated or the extent to which discussions could usefully be conducted around a common table. In Sweden, where the techniques of labor mediation have probably been developed and refined further than in any other industrialized country, the mediator, following an initial joint meeting, conducts his negotiations separately with the parties.

In the more difficult conflicts a mediator or a mediating commission must in the initial stage exercise a great deal of ingenuity. Sometimes one of the parties may take exception to something which otherwise would be of a comparatively minor character. Ralph Bunche has told of the difficulty caused in one of the first meetings attempted at Rhodes when one of the parties refused to shake hands. The meeting was promptly adjourned and the problem surmounted later when as guests of Dr. Bunche in his personal quarters at the hotel the party in question could not be so impolite as to refuse to greet his other guests. It was only then possible to proceed with discussions.

**Building up of confidence.** If the mediation effort has been wisely launched the parties to the dispute will enter the discussions with, at the least, an indifferent attitude toward the mediator or the commission, and possibly at the best, a general expectancy and a sense of relief that someone else has now attempted settlement. The mediatory body must proceed to build up the confidence of the parties in its impartiality and in its ability to understand each party's case and the fundamental nature of the issues in conflict. In difficult labor and international disputes, confidence in the mediator or commission is often accelerated by the mediator or commission getting firsthand knowledge of the problems which caused the dispute. The general means through which confidence is established would appear to be the same in both fields.

**Factual deflation.** This would appear to be another standard requirement of any mediation effort. It is not only something attempted by an especially assigned mediator or commission in the more intimate negotiations, but it is often a result of the parties' own give and take in negotiations conducted through the mediator or under his chairmanship.

The principle is frequently utilized by a governmental or intergovernmental authority in an effort to deflate rival claims, get at the true facts in the case, and, if necessary, present these to the public. Commissions of investigation have been appointed occasionally by the United Nations previous to a dispute being submitted to mediation. While the primary function of these commissions has been to bring back a report on the nature and scope of the conflict, their reports have usually helped to counteract the exaggerated public claims of the parties in conflict.

We have noted the creation by the General Assembly of a standing Peace Observation Commission. The theory behind the Commission is that in a situation of tension or conflict the availability of a prompt third-party report might be a distinct aid to efforts at settlement.

National governments have frequently resorted to fact-finding boards in labor disputes in an effort to get an impartial appraisal before the public. In this case, however, the board is more frequently appointed after initial efforts at mediation have failed.

**Raising doubts about positions already assumed.** As exaggeration and misunderstanding are removed from the immediate issues in dispute, mediators in both fields can usually move on to the task of widening out the perspective in which these issues are considered. Factors which had not previously been considered by the parties in their direct negotiations and which have a bearing on settlement can be introduced by the mediator or, with his encouragement, by one of the parties. Each case has its own differing characteristics, but the general principles would appear to be the same in any mediatory effort.

**Alternative solutions: expanding the area of agreement.** The means through which mediators in both fields develop and propose alternative solutions for the principal issues in dispute would appear to be very similar. They often find it useful in the initial stages to select out those simpler parts of the conflict and get these settled and out of the way. Occasionally no progress can be made until one or more of the major issues are tackled. The more serious problems usually occur, however, as the mediator attempts to expand an initial area of agreement to cover the more complex and fundamental issues.

We have suggested the advantages in labor disputes of making the initial presentations of alternative solutions to the parties separately. All too frequently, in both labor and international disputes, proposals are made to minds which are still unprepared for them. The advantages and disadvantages of alternative solutions can usually be considered with more freedom and more objectivity if the initial discussions on them take place separately between the mediator and the parties. We have noted the very human tendency, if such proposals are made first in a joint conference, for one party to reject the proposal if the other is inclined to accept it. The limitations of such an approach, however, go deeper. In serious conflicts it is likely that one or both parties, because of public statements which they have made, and because of commitments or aims, only some of which may be known to the mediator, may have difficulty in accepting any compromise solution. It is often only as the mediator tries out certain alternative solutions that he becomes aware of these previously unexpressed aims or commitments. The parties are much more likely, in direct and informal talks with the mediator, to enter into a frank discussion of the real problems they face and the difficulties which are presented by his proposals. If progress is to be made toward a solution, it is essential that the mediator give objective and sympathetic attention to these background problems faced by each side. Only thus will he be able to develop proposals sufficiently accommodated to the real situation faced by both parties to win their eventual assent.

It is thus in Sweden that the greater part of a mediation effort is conducted with the mediator meeting separately with the parties. This approach has much in common with the procedures used by the Commission on Indonesia, by Dr. Frank Graham in his work on Kashmir, and the use of technical experts followed by top-level visits to capitals as developed by Count Bernadotte and Ralph Bunche in Palestine. We have called attention to the final sifting out of the possible areas of agreement which resulted from the stream of proposals put forward by the latter in his Palestine mediation.

### COOLING-OFF PERIODS

*Cooling-off periods have proved to be of limited usefulness as a technique for preparing the way for agreement in major disputes.*

When William Jennings Bryan, as Secretary of State, proposed the use of fact-finding commissions in international affairs, he was suggesting the use of a procedure which has continued to demonstrate its effectiveness in facilitating a settlement in labor disputes and which has proved itself of similar usefulness in the international field. His suggestions with regard to cooling-off periods did not prove of equal value.

Experience in the labor field indicates that the "cooling-off" concept as originally propounded has very little validity. In an emotionally charged conflict, in which both sides believe that basic issues are at stake, the parties are unlikely to call off a strike or a lockout and to cool down during a period in which little or no effort is made at settlement. As we have noted in our discussion of labor disputes, when such a period is enforced on the parties they are just as likely to "heat up." The latest effort to utilize this concept in the handling of labor disputes in the United States is in the injunction period of emergency action under the Taft-Hartley Act. Here, as in other cases in which no adequate provision is made for continuing mediation during the cooling-off period, or in which no other thoroughgoing approach is made to relieve the basic tensions in the dispute, the concept has not proved itself particularly useful.

Occasionally in labor disputes a halt is called in mediation while the parties are asked to consider some proposal of the mediator or the mediation agency. The idea behind such a tactic, however, is scarcely the same as that behind cooling-off periods.

The continuing efforts to get a political settlement in Palestine illustrate a somewhat different and possibly more fruitful approach to a deadlock in settlement negotiations. At one point when the mediation commission reached an impasse an Economic Survey Mission was sent to the region. With Gordon Clapp, Chairman of the TVA, as its head, it made a survey and recommended economic measures designed to improve several of the economic and social situations which were an aggravation to the conflict. The mediating commission was kept in being during the period in which these measures were being carried out.

One type of situation in which the cooling-off concept might be useful would be a conflict in which the mediator or the mediating agency would conclude that the negotiators for one or both of the parties were taking positions which were substantially more intransigent than those of their associates in their own organization or their governments. In such cases a temporary halt in negotiations might be useful—although even in these cases it is likely that some proposals from the mediating agency for general study by the parties would be a helpful means of precipitating the necessary internal agreement.

### CONCLUDING THE AGREEMENT

*If settlement agreements are reached in informal meetings between the mediatory agency and the parties to the dispute, it is important to have these agreements carefully formulated and registered at a formal meeting.*

This generalization is so obvious that it scarcely needs documentation. Mediation efforts in both labor and international disputes profit from frequent informal discussions with the participants. Usually no minutes are kept of these meetings. However, if agreements are reached in such meetings it is most important that they be carefully recorded. International mediation experience indicates the desirability of convening promptly a formal meeting at which the agreement is approved. The time between the meetings is used for the careful drafting of the agreement and for the negotiators to bring their associates into line before the agreement is formalized.

Labor experience indicates a similar necessity of promptly and carefully recording the agreement. Whether it should be done at the meeting in which it is reached, or at a subsequent one, depends very largely on the authority of the negotiators for the parties in dispute and whether, in their judgment or in that of the mediator, it would be useful for them to consult their colleagues before making a final commitment.

# 6

---

## *Two Questions*

---

Out of any study of this kind several important questions are likely to emerge which are of a nature not permitting any preliminary conclusions. In this case, the first is a very practical one, relating to the development of the machinery for peaceful settlement in the United Nations. The second concerns the interrelation of the mediating and restraining functions of government.

### The Development of Permanent Mediation Machinery

Few people would hold that the present United Nations mediation machinery is as good as it can be made. In any efforts to improve it the following query is likely to emerge.

At what stage in the development of an intergovernmental institution is it useful to establish a "standing" mediatory agency having the freedom to offer its mediatory facilities on its own administrative motion, at the time when it believes such action would be most helpful in facilitating a settlement?

We have noted the creation within the United Nations of the Peace Observation Commission and the accompanying hope that by having facilities for fact finding promptly available in a serious dispute, hostilities might be forestalled and a basis more readily found for peaceful settlement. In the establishment of this Commission the United Nations has taken an important step forward in putting its peaceful settlement machinery on a "standing" basis.

We have noted also the establishment of the United Nations Panel on Inquiry and Conciliation—to which several governments have already nominated personnel. The creation of this roster and the responsibility assumed by governments to attempt to make the services of its members available to the United Nations, is intended to facilitate the selection and appointment of persons competent to serve the United Nations in a conciliation, mediation, or fact-finding capacity.

We have noted the great advantages of mediation agencies in the labor field having the freedom to offer their facilities, often on quite an informal basis, without the necessity of the type of legislative consideration which usually takes place in the United Nations. While industrial management in the United States strongly opposed initially the creation of a standing Federal agency having the freedom to offer its mediatory facilities on its own motion, this type of machinery has come to be generally accepted and has now demonstrated its usefulness.

It would obviously be both impossible and unwise to attempt to establish any comparable mediation machinery in the United Nations until a substantial number of governments had become sufficiently committed to both the principle and practice of

United Nations mediation that they would be prepared to accept the services of any additional machinery which might be created.

The institutional settings may be so different that no general parallel can exist with the facilities developed for mediation in the labor field. Both the Security Council and the General Assembly, however, have of late made more frequent use of the conciliatory services of their Presidents. On several occasions this informal initiative has been accepted by the parties in conflict. On the basis of the analysis presented in the study we would conclude that until the dissimilarity of the respective settings is further established, we are justified in suggesting that there may be some comparability in the types of machinery most suitable for mediation. We would therefore raise the question as to the stage in the growth of United Nations peacemaking activity when it would be useful to consider the further development within the United Nations of the facilities for informal mediation.

### Measures of Restraint

This has been primarily a study in the practices and techniques of mediation. As has been evident, however, these could not be considered adequately without constant reference to the institutional settings in which they were used.

Experience in labor mediation suggests that the growth of the institutions of government is an indispensable aid to the settlement of labor disputes. Mediation is usually undertaken by a special government agency. The symbol and the ever-present reality of the government, as the impartial guardian of the public interest, has been an unquestioned aid to the settlement of conflicts. Labor experience also suggests, however, that there is no easy answer as to how the government's political, legal, and police authority can be so used as to restrain hostilities and to facilitate the necessary agreement.

While the United States government in times of public emergency has through injunction or plant seizure frequently forced a resumption of production, it has not felt it was in a position to force a settlement of the issues in dispute on terms not acceptable to the parties. Sir Frederick Leggett and Carl Christian Schmidt have called attention to the difficulties the British and Swedish governments respectively have encountered in past efforts to force the acceptance of particular patterns of settlement. Dispute settlement has thus continued to rely to a very large extent on the techniques of mediation, even though more forceful means have been used to maintain production while the controversy remained unresolved. This is an important distinction not often enough recognized. Police force and legal punishment can be used to suppress violence, the government can take possession of a property, an injunction can even make it temporarily unlawful for an organized group to conduct a strike; but all of these remedies fail to make men work against their will. In a democracy, the only citizens who are forced to work are prisoners and drafted members of the military forces. Neither drafting nor imprisonment can be considered seriously as an acceptable antidote to a strike.

These same problems as to the proper and effective relationship between measures of restraint and measures of mediation are present in the international field. As is indicated by United Nations experience in Palestine, Indonesia, Kashmir, and Korea, they are among the most important of those faced by the world organization. We have noted the number of times the Security Council has used the methods of persuasion and mediation of Chapter VI of the United Nations Charter, in its efforts both to restrain hostilities and to gain a settlement, instead of attempting the more forceful type of action permitted by Chapter VII.

We have suggested the degree to which three of the leading

industrial countries in the Western world have found it necessary to develop the techniques of mediation and voluntary agreement as a means of settling industrial disputes—even those which have assumed a "public-emergency" character.

Has experience in the national community anything to contribute to these vastly more difficult questions in the international field? It would seem probable, but any defensible conclusions would require a more complete analysis.

This study, in the meantime, may have cast some light on the interrelationship between "measures of restraint" and the "art of peaceful settlement."

# APPENDIX I

---

## Provisions for the Handling of Industrial Disputes in the U.S.S.R.

### BY LOIS JANE STONE

---

### Settlement by Mixed Union-Management Commissions

The arrangements in the Soviet Union for the settlement of labor disputes are perhaps most comparable to the mixed commission of international practice. The basic organ is the so-called Appraisal and Conflicts Commission, or, from its initials in Russian, the RKK. This body is composed of representatives of the local labor organization in the factory or institution involved (the *zavmestkom*) and the representatives of the administration. It would appear to be permanently organized in those factories and institutions large enough to have a trade-union committee, and to be organized on an *ad hoc* basis in smaller factories. In especially large factories and institutions, where there are separate labor organizations for different shops and shifts, RKK's may be organized on that level, too, though there will also be a general RKK for the whole factory.[1] The representatives to the RKK are usually chosen by the trade union and by management. Their terms of appointment and the methods for choosing them are not determined by the legislation. In factories or in institutions where wage committees of the *zavmestkoms* are organized, the chairmen or vice-chairmen of these commissions represent the factory union in the RKK, but this appears to be custom and not law.[2]

The RKK may decide both justiciable and nonjusticiable disputes, that is, disputes involving rights protected by legislation and enforceable in the court system, and those involving changes in conditions of work and incidents not provided for by legislation which cannot be taken to court. Decisions which are unsatisfactory to either party may be appealed to the union hierarchy, which can review the case with the higher ranks of management. In cases of noncompliance with decisions of the RKK the courts are called upon to enforce the decisions, but not to review them.[3] As we shall indicate in more detail later, certain types of decisions can be appealed to the regional, and eventually to the central, trade-union organization. In the U.S.S.R. the central union organization carries out some of the administrative functions which are handled by governmental ministries of labor in other countries.

A 1949 pamphlet states that "All labor disputes are resolved either in the RKK . . . or in court, or by administrative means."[4] However, this was not always the case, and a cursory

---

[1]N. G. Aleksandrov and G. K. Moskalenko, *Sovetskoe trudovoe pravo*, p. 276.

[2]N. G. Aleksandrov and D. M. Genkin, *Sovetskoe trudovoe pravo*, p. 314.

[3]D. V. Shveitser, *Razreshenie trudovykh sporov v S S S R*, pp. 16–21.

[4]*Ibid.*, p. 14.

reading of the code of legislation concerning labor might lead to a different conclusion. This code went into effect on November 15, 1922, and naturally contains traces of the changes which the Soviet economy has undergone since that time.[5] It provides, in addition to the methods mentioned above, for settlement by means of Courts of Conciliation and also by arbitral tribunals.[6] Courts of Conciliation were composed of representatives of the parties appointed *ad hoc*, and of a president, named by the Labor Inspection. The president could not decide the question, but assisted in working out a settlement satisfactory to the parties. The role of the president appears to have been very similar to that of a mediator in United States labor disputes.

The distinction between the jurisdiction of these Courts of Conciliation and of the RKK is not clear.[7] According to a 1936 text the position of the Courts of Conciliation was insignificant. "In practice, questions not receiving settlement in the RKK or in the conclusion of the collective contract, do not receive, in large part, settlement in Courts of Conciliation and are transferred to an arbitral tribunal." The Courts thus were superfluous, serving only to lengthen and complicate the process of settling labor disputes.[8] By 1938 cases not settled in the RKK were no longer appealed to the Courts of Conciliation.[9] Apparently both they and the arbitral tribunals ceased to exist in 1937.[10]

It would appear that labor disputes are now handled in three ways, depending on the issues in dispute and on the personnel

[6]Aleksandrov and Genkin, *op. cit.*, p. 86.

[6]*Zakonodatelstvo o trude. Kommentariy.* N. G. Aleksandrov, E. I. Astrakhan, S. S. Karinsky, G. K. Moskalenko, p. 248.

[7]Z. Z. Grishin, *Sovetskoe trudovoe pravo*, p. 223.

[8]*Ibid.*, pp. 223–224.

[9]K. P. Gorshenin, R. P. Orlov, Ya. A. Karasov (eds.) *Sovetskoe trudovoe pravo*, p. 87.

[10]Aleksandrov and Moskalenko, *op. cit.*, p. 227.

which is involved. Certain types of disputes and cases involving certain classes of workers do not go to the RKK or to the People's Court, but are appealed through an administrative arrangement, within the industry concerned. Conflicts in connection with disciplinary penalties, imposed under certain legislation, are dealt with on this basis, as are conflicts in connection with dismissal at the demand of the union, and dismissals based on orders of the Ministry of State Control. Also workers in the transportation and communication industries must take their demands through these channels, and workers classified as "responsible" according to a list of categories in legislation from 1929,[11] cannot take cases involving their dismissals either to the People's Court or the RKK.

Among such workers are included elected workers, occupying paid positions in the organizations electing them, members of boards managing a long series of institutions and directors of such institutions, private secretaries to the directors of such institutions, directors of the local branches of such institutions, and the authorized agents of various political organizations. Also included on the list are many other officials whose posts have economic significance, including those who head divisions of enterprises which do not have legal personality but are managed on a basis of independent economic accounting (*khozraschet*). Responsible editors of periodicals, technical directors or chief engineers, foremen and men corresponding to them in enterprises, officials responsible for fire brigades in factories and for confidential (security) units and divisions, chief and senior accountants, and superintendents of factories and those of divisions of factories who have their own offices also may not take their complaints concerning dismissal to the RKK or to the People's Court. Generally speaking, anyone who has the right to hire and fire other

[11]*Zakonodatelstvo*, pp. 243–244.

employees may be dismissed without recourse to the procedures outlined above. However, if the higher organs of the industry recognize their dismissal as unjust such employees may present suits to recover back pay. The commentary on the code continues after outlining these provisions: "The list of categories of responsible workers, established by the NKT (People's Commissariat of Labor), whose cases concerning dismissal and restoration to employment ought not to be examined in the RKK and in the People's Court . . . is not subject to broad interpretation."[12]

All other cases may be referred to the RKK. Disputes which must first be referred to the RKK include those involving the transfer of a worker from one job to another; payment for underproduction in comparison to the norms set and for the production of defective goods; dismissal from work for unsuitability for the work to be performed, and for the nonfulfillment of obligations in connection with the work; compensation for the use of tools, belonging to the worker; distribution of special clothing and special food allowances, and in certain circumstances monetary compensation for them; application of an abridged work day and of lengthened vacations; payment for the execution of work of a different qualification as a substitute; payment for layoffs; payment for preparation for piecework; deductions from the workers' salary for damages to the enterprise caused by him in the execution of his duties (in those cases for which the law establishes a limited liability and which are not in the exclusive competence of the court); payments for vacations which are not taken; payment for probation periods; bonus payments due a worker; payment for overtime work; and help in the living expenses of a worker in connection with the nonfulfillment of obligations due under a labor contract.

[12]*Ibid.*, pp. 245–246.

In most other cases (except those listed for administrative treatment) the worker has the option of first presenting his case to the RKK or of taking it directly to the People's Court. The commentary on the code gives as an example of the sort of case which may go either to the RKK or to the People's Court a conflict concerning a dismissal made in order to cut the staff of the enterprise. While the RKK has jurisdiction over conflicts involving workers and employees employed in enterprises, institutions, and farms in which there are no union members,[13] such conflicts may also be taken to the People's Court.[14]

The RKK has no jurisdiction over questions concerning changes in official salaries, established by the state, and over those concerning the granting of living space to employees, except as provided for by contract. (In the Soviet Union much of the housing is controlled by the economic enterprises which grant it to employees. Since wages are paid in large part on the basis of state directives, a good apartment has served occasionally in the past to lure experts from other enterprises.)

In the mid-thirties it appeared that one of the main tasks of the RKK was its jurisdiction over the collective contract, as "one of the levers in the struggle for the socialist organization of labor." "The tendency of the development of the RKK in the passing years consists in the ever great extension of the functions of the RKK and the transference to the latter of a significant quantity of the labor disputes arising in industry."[15]

### The Growth of ·Legislation

By 1947 things had changed considerably, for legislation now covered many points earlier left to settlement by the parties.

[13]*Ibid.,* p. 248.
[14]*Ibid.,* p. 249.
[15]Grishin, *op. cit.,* pp. 219–220.

Earlier, when the conditions of labor of workers and employees were regulated in a significant measure by collective contracts, such conflicts (nonjusticiable) arose chiefly on the conclusion, and also in the process of execution of collective contracts. At the present time, when conditions of labor of workers and employees are defined in basic legislation, nonjusticiable conflicts arise in connection with questions not receiving exhaustive decision in the legislation concerning labor and decided either in the collective contracts or by agreement of the administration with the worker or the union, or on the basis of an order of the administration, subject to approval of the union.[16]

According to the original rules of procedure of the RKK, it may set the norms of payment, piecework rates, and so forth, but in 1933 an order of the All Union Central Council of Unions ordered that the RKK confine its proceedings to the determination of the legality of the norms of payment, not actually ascertaining them itself.[17] It is evident from this that, however broad remains the competence of the RKK at the present day, its operations have been much curtailed since the time of the first five-year plan, largely in all likelihood because of the operations of such plans. Now a "wage bill" is set for a whole industry by plan, and general classifications of workers are set up, as in a civil service system. There is no longer much place left for general negotiations at the plant level on such questions, and it is on the plant level that the RKK operates.

### Operation of the Appraisal and Conflicts Commissions (RKK)

Because of the informal character of its deliberations, there is not much information generally available concerning the organization of the RKK. As a body it has a chairman and a secretary,

[16]Aleksandrov and Moskalenko, *op. cit.,* p. 275.
[17]*Ibid.,* p. 277.

chosen at each meeting for the subsequent one. At one meeting the chairman will be from the union and the secretary from management. At the next the positions will be reversed. The officials are charged with the convocation of the next meeting and the preparation of the agenda. The administration of the factory or institution bears the cost of the correspondence carried on by the RKK and provides storage space for its effects and accommodations for its meetings. Meetings take place in the free time of those involved, the time of the meeting being established by agreement of the *fabzavmestkom* with the administration. If the factory or institution is working two or three shifts, the time for the meetings is arranged so that the representatives of the workers' side who are needed at the given meeting can attend in their free time. The workers also are not supposed to prepare their cases during working hours. Meetings of the RKK are attended by the workers involved, and those who are permanent participants, *i.e.,* the staff of the RKK. No one is paid for attending the meetings. If a worker desires he may challenge one of the regular members of the RKK as being unfit to participate in the case being heard. A committee of workers and employees will decide the justness of a challenge in relation to one of their representatives on the Commission. Administration will likewise decide the justness of a challenge to one of its representatives on the Commission.[18]

Any worker or member of the administration may appeal to the RKK over a believed infringement of rights or over an assumed failure to live up to obligations by the other party. The local union committee has the right to present to the RKK disputes involving either separate workers or all the workers in the plant. The administration must consult with the RKK before firing a worker because of inability to perform his allotted function, or before enforcing deductions from a worker's

[18]*Zakonodatelstvo*, pp. 252–253.

salary, in compensation for injury inflicted by him on the enterprise.[19]

As indicated above, the RKK no longer has jurisdiction over the collective contract, which is under the jurisdiction of higher labor-union organizations and corresponding industrial organizations. It also does not have jurisdiction over certain disputes which are settled by administrative action.[20] It may not entertain claims of workers who have not previously attempted to settle the dispute by means of direct negotiations with the administration.[21] Shop and shift RKK's in general have the same jurisdiction (which will be further defined) as the general factory RKK's, but they may not handle cases concerning the transfer of a worker to other work outside the given shop, dismissals made in order to curtail staff, or applications for a shortened workday and lengthened vacations.[22]

Among the nonjusticiable disputes now coming within the jurisdiction of the general factory RKK are those which relate to the placing of a worker within a tariff schedule. In every industry in the U.S.S.R. there are schedules which approximate civil service tables. Workers are classified and within each grouping a certain range of salaries may be paid. It is, of course, impossible to set up a table which will provide for every gradation of skill and for all the possible occupations and degrees of responsibility which are encountered in industry. So the system apparently provides its share of dispute cases.[23] The RKK also examines conflicts in connection with the establishment and change of conditions of labor defined in a contract, it establishes

---

[19]Shveitser, *op. cit.*, p. 16.

[20]*Ibid.*, p. 17.

[21]*Zakonodatelstvo*, p. 252.

[22]*Ibid.*, p. 254.

[23]Aleksandrov and Genkin, *op. cit.*, p. 314.

the necessity of overtime work, and it institutes arrangements giving regular and special vacations, and settles questions concerning the payment of monetary compensation for vacations not taken.[24]

Disputes relating to dismissals must be brought before the RKK within a period of 14 days after the dismissal, and also cases involving deductions from earnings to which a worker objects. Cases involving disputes concerning payment for overtime work must be brought before the RKK within a month, and all remaining cases within three months. In exceptional cases and for important reasons the RKK may consider cases brought after the time has lapsed. These short periods were not always provided by law, but experience showed that with longer periods there was a tendency for claims to pile up, and for the examination of each case to be prolonged. It appears that at some times as much as a year or two, and even more, has elapsed before cases concerning overtime pay have come before various RKK's, and it proved exceedingly difficult to ascertain the facts after such a lapse of time.[25]

The trial of a case in the RKK begins with a declaration by the person, usually the worker involved, in which he states his claim. If either side contests the facts alleged in the declaration, or if the whole claim seems in need of some substantiation, the RKK consults the documents involved or examines witnesses, and in appropriate cases consults experts, for instance to verify the qualifications of the worker. After the Commission has consulted all the relevant evidence it attempts to reach a settlement to which both sides can agree. To ensure the independence of the representatives of the local union organization in the RKK, the law does not per-

[24]Aleksandrov and Moskalenko, *op. cit.*, p. 277. See also *Zakonodatelstvo*, pp. 242–243.

[25]Shveitser, *op. cit.*, pp. 17–18.

mit their dismissal from work without a special agreement with the higher union organizations.[26]

Conflicts which appear to be of a justiciable nature, not settled in the RKK because of a failure of the parties to reach an agreement, may later be taken to the People's Court of the local jurisdiction. Those conflicts of a nonjusticiable nature which are taken first to the RKK but which are not settled there usually become a matter of negotiation between the higher union and management officials.[27]

Since the decisions of the RKK are reached by joint agreement there is little difficulty in enforcing them, but occasionally the administration refuses to carry out a decision, apparently most often in cases involving monetary payments. In order to enforce such a decision the union representative must first take it to the regional or central committee of the union involved. That organ then verifies the legality of the action previously taken by the RKK and refers the question to a People's Court. If the sum involved was fixed in monetary units, the People's Court enforces it as it stands, without any further review of the legality of the decision. If, however, the exact sum in money is not fixed in the decision, for instance, if the RKK has ordered the administration to pay two weeks' wages to the worker involved, the Court then conducts an inquiry to determine the exact sum. In no case does the People's Court, in executing a decision of the RKK, examine its legality.[28] Decrees or orders issued by the higher union authorities on their own and not constituting part of a decision of the RKK, cannot be carried out by such an arrangement.[29] Higher court appeals may be taken, but, as is the case in most continental

[26]*Ibid.*, pp. 18–19.

[27]Aleksandrov and Genkin, *op. cit.*, p. 314.

[28]Shveitser, *op. cit.*, pp. 19–20.

[29]*Zakonodatelstvo*, p. 255.

countries, judicial review is a somewhat different process from
that in the United States. The judges are limited to ascertaining
whether the decision reached was in accord with existing legislation.

Substantive decisions of shop and shift RKK's may be appealed
to the general factory RKK, but if the general factory RKK does
not annul the decision of the lower body, that decision stands.
Substantive decisions of the general factory RKK and also decisions of the shop and shift RKK's which have not been annulled
may be appealed to the regional committee of the union, and decisions of the regional (*oblast* or *krai*) committee, to the central
committee. Decisions of the central committee of the union are
final.

Decisions of the RKK can be reopened by higher union authorities only if they provide for a deterioration in the conditions
of work as set by law or contract; for exceeding the maximum
norms set by law or contract; for the infringement of rules concerning the organization and limits of competence of the RKK
(if such an infringement is reflected in the substance of the case);
if the decision was based on falsified documents or false testimony,
and the fact can be established by indisputable proofs; and if
circumstances are disclosed which remained unknown to the
RKK but are essential to a just decision of the case. Also a decision may be reopened if it purports to settle a case, already
under examination in the People's Court, or settled by that organ.
In any of these cases the previous decision may be questioned by
higher union authorities, but they may not themselves reach a
new decision. The case must be remanded for a new examination
either to the People's Court or to the RKK involved. The Proc-
urator may enter the proceedings at any point, either to protest
a decision already made or to assist in the examination of a
case. In passing it might be noted that if a monetary sum is

paid to a worker under the original decision of the RKK, and that decision is later annulled, he is not obliged to repay the enterprise, unless the decision was annulled on the grounds that it was based on false information or false documents supplied by him.[30]

Even if the worker elects to take his case initially to the People's Court or if the case is referred by the RKK to the People's Court, the normal procedure for civil cases is not followed. In the first place no written brief need be presented. The worker may make an oral declaration of his claim, and the People's Judge draws up a protocol from the remarks of the plaintiff which is entered in the records. Imposts and court expenses normally charged in civil cases are waived in cases involving labor disputes, and since the union is obligated to provide its members with free legal aid workers need not incur any expenses in presenting their cases to the court. All labor cases, regardless of the amount involved, are tried in the nearest People's Court, though normal civil cases are often referred to more distant People's Courts which handle cases concerning sums of the magnitude involved. Labor cases are also tried in the People's Court on a limited time schedule, to hasten decisions and to assure that the trial is held while the facts are still clear in the minds of the witnesses. A further step in the "struggle with red tape" is the provision that if a member of the administration fails to appear to testify in a case the court may order the local militia (corresponding to our police) to bring him to court. Immediate execution of the decision is permitted, even if appeals are filed, an exception from the general rule. However, in the process of review of the decision by the higher courts, if the courts feel that the original decision was unjust and that the People's Court had before it all the relevant evidence, in contrast to the higher labor

[30]*Ibid.*, pp. 254–255.

organs, the higher court may hand down a new and binding decision.[31]

## Summary

In the opinion of Soviet authors there are many advantages to settling disputes in the Appraisal and Conflicts Commissions (RKK). One describes them thus:

1. The RKK is founded in the enterprise itself or the institution and in the large enterprises—in the shops, that is, in the very place where a labor dispute arises. The closeness of the RKK to the origin of the dispute secures rapid treatment in this commission, and consequently rapid examination of the dispute without unnecessary waste of time.

2. The RKK is organized from representatives of the local union organization and local administration, that is, from people who well know the conditions of production and all those circumstances in which quarrels arise. This doubtless influences the quality of examination of the dispute, since people, knowing the concrete circumstances of the given industry and its specifications, can better analyze a dispute and consequently decide it justly.

3. Treatment in the RKK is not bound by any formalities and the arrangement itself of trial of the cases is free of intricate procedural rules.

4. The conciliatory character of the trial of cases in the RKK signifies that the decision of disputes is a result of the voluntary agreement of the parties. The participation of the union in the settlement of disputes in the RKK is also a beneficial characteristic of this organ.[32]

Though this treatment of the subject is by no means exhaustive, certain clear differences between this system and that of

[31]Shveitser, *op. cit.*, pp. 22–23.

[32]Shveitser, *op. cit.*, p. 15.

most other countries emerge. In part they are a consequence of a
planned economy, where there is no place for the sort of en-
lightened self-interest which our union leaders as well as our
businessmen pursue. The general effect of much of the *Legislation Concerning Labor* is of a sort of civil service system, though
it seems odd at one place in the list to note that factory foremen
are considered responsible workers, whose claims concerning dismissal from employment cannot be heard in the ordinary arrangement, whereas teachers in middle schools are not.[33] This difference in practice is reflected by a difference in theory. Lenin once
said:

> In the field of disagreements and conflicts of separate groups of the
> working class with separate institutions and organs of the workers'
> state the task of unions is to further the most rapid and painless settle-
> ment of conflicts with the maximum benefits for the working groups
> represented by them, since these benefits can be carried out not to the
> injury of other groups and without harm to the development of the
> workers' state and its economy as a whole, for only this development
> can found the basis for the material and spiritual well-being of the
> working class.[34]

Also significant is the fact that the Soviet Union has since 1933
been without any equivalent of our Department of Labor, the
Narkomtrud having then been abolished, and that most of its
functions, including the supervision of the actions of the RKK,
have been taken over by the regular trade union organizations.[35]

A Soviet jurist expressed the difference thus, last year:

> Labor disputes in the U.S.S.R., in distinction from labor conflicts
> in capitalist countries, arise not on the ground of class conflicts, but as
> a result of the infringement of laws by separate leaders of institutions

[33]*Zakonodatelstvo*, pp. 245–246.

[34]Aleksandrov and Genkin, *op. cit.*, p. 312.

[35]*Ibid.*

and enterprises, or by separate workers and employees. The infringement of laws concerning labor leads to a labor dispute. Sometimes labor disputes arise because of insufficient understanding of labor legislation by separate administrators of enterprises (institutions) or by workers.

Labor disputes arise neither from the same causes nor do they have the same forms in the Soviet Union as in capitalist countries.[36]

It is notable that in this pamphlet the author carefully uses different words for disputes arising in capitalist countries, using the mild *spor* for labor disputes in the Soviet Union.

In all the books on labor disputes there is no mention of any process approaching mediation as it is practiced in the international sphere and in capitalist countries. The intervention of the Labor Inspection in appointing chairmen for the old Courts of Conciliation seems the closest approach, but even then, it was the intervention of one branch of the government to mediate between two other branches. There are not largely independent, autonomous economic organizations in the Soviet Union which set the stage for governmental mediatory intervention on behalf of the public interest. The RKK in its activities is an approach to an instrument of mediation, but there are limitations to the cases it can handle, and its sphere of action is bounded by the particular enterprise or factory. However, it is quite possible to exaggerate the differences, for even in the West the growth of labor legislation places limits on the labor and collective contracts, and any increase in socialized industry and in planning would place further restrictions on the content of labor contracts at the lower level.

BIBLIOGRAPHY

N. G. Aleksandrov, E. I. Astrakhan, S. S. Karinsky, and G. K. Moskalenko, *Zakonodatelstvo o trude. Kommentariy.* (*Legislation con-*

[36]Shveitser, *op. cit.*, pp. 11–12.

*cerning labor. Commentary*), Yuridicheskoe Izdatelstvo Ministerstva Yustitsii S S S R, Moskva, 1947.

N. G. Aleksandrov and D. M. Genkin, *Sovetskoe trudovoe pravo (Soviet labor law*), Yuridicheskoe Izdatelstvo N.K.Yu. S S S R, Moskva, 1946.

N. G. Aleksandrov and G. K. Moskalenko, *Sovetskoe trudovoe pravo* (*Soviet labor law*), Yuridicheskoe Izdatelstvo Ministerstva Yustitsii S S S R, Moskva, 1947.

K. P. Gorshenin, R. P. Orlov, and Ya. A. Karasev (editors), *Sovetskoe trudovoe pravo* (*Soviet labor law*), Moskva, 1938.

Z. Z. Grishin, *Sovetskoe trudovoe pravo* (*Soviet labor law*), O.G.I.Z., Moskva, 1936.

D. V. Shveitser, *Razreshenie trudovykh sporov v S S S R* (*The settlement of labor disputes in the U.S.S.R.*), Izdatelstvo "*Pravda*," Moskva, 1949.

# APPENDIX II

---

## *Some Suggestions for Social Science Research*

---

This study of mediation has grown out of an exchange of experience among a group largely composed of persons with practical experience in mediation. The tentative conclusions are those suggested by an initial review of experience in the two fields. These conclusions can be tested out in practice by mediators in both the labor and international fields. But is there any way of reaching more precise conclusions by using the as yet very imperfect methods of social science research?

It is possible that the many human, economic, and political variables will prevent the reaching of any conclusions having greater validity than those resulting from this pragmatic analysis. On the other hand, the weight of events which hangs in the balance when mediation is attempted may warrant further explorations of this kind, even if the chances of success seem small. Further research might invalidate some of these tentative conclusions, or might suggest other more important questions as yet unasked. While it might be easier to conduct this research in the labor field, it would be important for parallel, even if more limited, explorations to be conducted in the international field.

The manuscript was shown to a man with wide experience in the researching of human relations problems and he was asked what research problems, if any, could be developed from this material. What follows is based largely upon his replies.

The scientific method is subject to severe limitations in any study of this kind. The laboratory method must be ruled out, for those things which make mediation difficult cannot be reproduced synthetically. There are limitations to the statistical method because there are so many different types of situations, each containing within itself a complex of factors. A simple addition of cases would not be of value. Aspects of all three methods, however, might be used in combination to increase our understanding of the mediation process.

The objectives of such research would be to explore, in so far as present knowledge and methods will permit, some of the questions that have been raised. There are three broad areas in which research might be undertaken: (1) the measurement of the effect of mediation techniques now generally in use; (2) the development and teaching of mediation techniques; (3) an analysis of the effect on the mediation process of measures of restraint (emergency procedures) undertaken by the government.

This research could be facilitated by a much more complete survey of current experience, in conjunction with the development of methods for reporting this experience in a useful form. Some steps for getting research of this type under way are suggested below:

1. *Experiments with conference techniques*
   There has been a great deal of research done on conference techniques. To cite just a few examples: The Estes method of round

table discussion, role playing, democratic leadership toward problem solving. In this connection note should be taken of the Unesco report on *The Technique of International Conferences,* published on February 19, 1951. (UNESCO/SS/3.) A group of mediators might be asked to select those parts of this research believed to be most relevant to their mediation experience. The same men or others might then be asked, at their own discretion, to test out a set of propositions and to report on the results.

2. *Major factors influencing a willingness to compromise*

The rigidity with which a negotiator clings to his position fluctuates during the course of negotiations. The technique and the personal and governmental prestige of the mediator may be among the lesser influences playing upon the parties. The evaluation of relative bargaining strength, the fear of a strike or of open conflict, the ability to compromise without losing one's followers, the pressure of other interested groups, all play a major role in "conditioning" the parties. A more thorough analysis might be made of several mediation efforts in an effort to estimate the relationship of the principal power factors to the willingness of the parties to compromise.

3. *Responsibility of the mediator for the result*

Should the mediator have any goal other than an agreement? What if he believes the agreement to have within it the seeds of future trouble, to be unfair, or to be against the public interest? Is there any consensus of opinion among mediators as to their responsibility to the "public interest" for the type of agreement which is reached?

4. *Role of public debate*

There is a scale of public debate running from private negotiations publicly reported, through open discussions complete with television coverage. Certain general gradations on the scale might be established and the relationship of these gradations to a series of mediation efforts studied.

5. *The issuance of recommendations*

*a.* What is the effect of recommendations from a mediatory or fact-finding body on (1) the parties; (2) the public; (3) the course of negotiations?

  *b.* Can the form of written recommendations be improved? The present pattern in labor disputes is to issue fairly legal documents. (See Fact-finding reports, Atomic Panel reports, Railway Board reports.)

  *c.* Should recommendations be circulated and explained by the mediator? The present practice in labor is for fact finders to write a report and fade away.

6. *Teaching mediation skills*

  *a.* Are there teachable skills? If so, what are they?

  *b.* Such teaching might grow out of a study of the following general items:

  (1) Discussion techniques . . . role playing.

  (2) An elementary human relations awareness.

  (3) Listening skill.

  (4) A check list of techniques developed by mediators.

  (5) The historical background of dispute settlement—in the labor movement, in the League of Nations, in the United Nations.

  *c.* Such study could then be related to the mediation of a specific dispute through a study of:

  (1) The personal background (character, political ties, viewpoints of the key negotiators).

  (2) The factual background (wage data, contract clauses prevalent in industry, treaties, dispute history, etc.).

7. *Selection of mediators*

  Do successful mediators have certain qualities in common? If so, what are they?

8. *Measures of restraint (emergency procedures) in labor disputes*

  In a democracy, there is no absolute way to prevent a strike by legal or police force, because men at work against their will is slavery. The closest approach in the United States is convict labor in prisons, and military service of reluctant draftees. Neither of these methods is applicable to industrial production. The mediation process itself is influenced, however, by the type of emergency procedures that are established and that are kept in readiness in the event that agreement is not reached. Since these emergency procedures are far from a sure protection against strikes, more attention should be paid to their effect on mediation in order that the most favorable framework can be provided within which negotiations can take place.

The methods known and available to the government are these:

a. *Government seizure:* The effect of this is to transfer the workers into government service. The transfer is largely a legal fiction, nevertheless the fiction is ordinarily respected by the men. This does not settle a dispute, it merely postpones a strike while negotiations continue. To strike against the Federal government is supposedly illegal—and at any rate is considered revolutionary. But is there not a danger that if this method of strike prevention be used too often, the legal fiction will wear thin? A survey of the attitude of the men working under government seizure might yield useful information to the policy makers.

b. *Injunction:* An injunction also serves only to postpone strikes, it does not in itself achieve settlement. In many respects it is similar to government seizure, but it is usually far less palatable to labor—for it has the appearance of being aimed at labor alone rather than at both sides. Further research might be conducted on the role of injunctions in preventing disastrous strikes.

c. *Compulsory arbitration:* Compulsory arbitration can sometimes provide a solution to the dispute, but it will not necessarily yield a satisfactory one. The practice of mediation, under the threat of compulsory arbitration if mediation breaks down, requires further study. What methods can be devised to keep the weaker party from forcing the discussion into the hands of the arbitral body? Can certain items, such as wages, be isolated for compulsory arbitration, leaving other items open for negotiation? While the logical answer to this appears to be "no," this is the trend of thinking today in the United States Congress.

Are there any other strike-prevention techniques which can be devised?

Could similar research be undertaken into the relationship between the mediatory and the restraining functions in international affairs?

This section suggests in the most preliminary way some of the further research which might be undertaken in the mediation field. Skilled observation and analysis in the past has proven to be of great value in discovering common denominators in human behavior. The art of mediation can obviously not be reduced to rules laid down by the social scientist. Explorations of this kind, however, might put more refined and dependable tools into the hands of the artist.

# Index